DIGITAL
Wizardry

DIGITAL *Wizardry*

CREATIVE PHOTOSHOP TECHNIQUES

BRYAN ALLEN

With a Foreword by
MICHAEL J. McNAMARA

AMPHOTO BOOKS
An Imprint of Watson-Guptill Publications/New York

To my parents, who always made me feel like anything was possible; to my loving and supportive wife, Maribeth, a talented photographer herself; and to my stepson, Paul, whose creative energies will one day make me look like a first-year art student.

THIS PRODUCT IS NOT ENDORSED OR SPONSORED BY ADOBE SYSTEMS INCORPORATED.

Illustration Credits

Adobe® Photoshop® screen captures appear courtesy of Adobe Systems Incorporated.

Adobe and Photoshop are trademarks of Adobe Systems Incorporated.

Bryce 2, Painter 5, and Paint Alchemy screen captures appear courtesy of MetaCreations.

FotoQuote screen captures appear courtesy of Cradoc Corporation. © 1997 Cradoc Corporation.

Live Picture screen captures appear courtesy of Live Picture, Inc. © 1993–1997 Live Picture, Inc.

QuicKeys illustration © 1987–94, 1996–97 CE Software, Inc.

Speed Disk and Disk Doctor are part of Norton Utilities, made by Symantec.

Findit, a utility that comes with every Zip or Jazz drive, is made by Iomega.

First published in 1998 in the United States by Amphoto Books, an imprint of Watson-Guptill Publications, a division of BPI Communications,1515 Broadway, New York, N.Y. 10036

Library of Congress Cataloging-in-Publication Data

Allen, Bryan, 1960–
    Digital wizardry : creative Photoshop techniques / Bryan Allen.
       p.   cm.
    Includes bibliographical references and index.
    ISBN 0-8174-3797-5
    1. Computer graphics. 2. Adobe Photoshop. I. Title.
T385.A455 1998
006.6'869—dc21   98-5974
                           CIP

Manufactured in Hong Kong

First printing, 1998

1 2 3 4 5 6 7 8 9 / 06 05 04 03 02 01 00 99 98

Senior Editor: Robin Simmen
Editor: Victoria Craven
Designer: Jay Anning
Graphic Production: Hector Campbell

ACKNOWLEDGMENTS

They say that when the student is ready the teacher appears. I have been fortunate to have had several good mentors throughout my career.

When I was young and just starting out, Ralph Bogertman, a uniquely talented and creative photographer from New York City, took me in as his assistant and taught me how to be a photographer and to think for myself.

Bob Krist, known as "The Great One" among the lucky few who have worked with him, picked up where Ralph left off and did his level best to push me up.

Wayne Roth saw something in me, when I was a young and eager photographer, and brought me to the next level. We had a partnership for a time called "Chiselvision" and together we produced a terrific body of work (much of which appears in this book).

All three of these men were more generous and giving of their time and energies than I ever had a right to expect. I thank them all.

CONTENTS

FOREWORD

The world of photography is changing faster today than anyone could have imagined a decade ago. Computers, digital cameras, scanners, electronic printers, on-line World Wide Web services, and even digital video cameras are now as much a part of the photographic experience as film, processing, and interchangeable lenses. These new electronic tools enable photographers to capture and review images instantly, send photos around the world in minutes instead of days, and even record sound along with their still photos. But nothing has caused us to change the way we take photographs, and look at photographs, as much as digital imaging software, which allows us to alter photographic reality in ways darkroom technicians could only dream about twenty years ago. Among these programs one stands head and shoulders above the rest—Adobe Photoshop. Since its official introduction in 1990, Photoshop has become the most successful digital imaging software program of our time. It has helped spawn a new breed of photographers who worry less about getting the shot right the first time because they plan to manipulate their work to perfection on the computer. Older photographers may cringe at the thought that capturing the moment is no longer the goal it used to be, but most will admit that using a program like Photoshop to help retouch scratched originals or liberate their creative vision in the comfort of a well-lit, ventilated room is far better than spending hours inhaling dangerous chemical fumes in a traditional darkroom.

Prior to Photoshop's official arrival on the scene, a time many consider the digital dark ages, there were only a handful of digital imaging programs designed for use on desktop computers. Most of these were so expensive, slow, and limiting that computer-savvy photographers often found it easier to write their own software code to produce the effects they wanted. At the same time, powerful desktop computers were also extremely expensive and as slow as snails by today's standards, so the very idea of using the computer as a "digital darkroom" was foreign to all but those in the publishing world who could afford high-end, and high-priced, systems. Photoshop changed all that by becoming the first program under $1,000 to offer features such as the Cloning Tool, the Magic Wand, and a slew of other features we now find in entry-level programs selling for $100 or less. By and large, early adopters of Photoshop were professional photographers who were looking for a faster way to retouch photos and create digital art. In order to "go digital," it took these pioneers a significant investment in time, computer equipment, scanners, and output devices. But even back then, Photoshop gurus were few in number, and most of those were known by their outstanding work that rose above mere technical proficiency and expressed a unique vision. Over the years Photoshop has grown in complexity and power, and now offers so many features and tools that it's nearly impossible to master them all. On top of that, hundreds of special effects "plug-in" filters are sold by companies riding the Photoshop wave, and a variety of three-dimensional, catalog, and paint programs offer features that enhance the Photoshop experience. Meanwhile, high-speed computers have dropped dramatically in price, as did film and flatbed scanners, digital cameras, and photo-quality desktop printers (many of which are bundled with free versions of Photoshop). As a result, just about anyone can become a digital photographer or learn Photoshop. To meet the ever-growing demand for instruction in the secrets of this amazing program, nearly every graphic arts college, and many high schools, offer Photoshop courses and seminars. Every year there are thousands of young Photoshop "technicians" flooding the market who know how to use Photoshop tools and shortcuts, but not when to use them. They have yet to learn that real artistry comes from within and that Photoshop can be used to express it. That's why Bryan Allen's *Digital Wizardry* should stand out among the throngs of Photoshop tutorials lining the shelves in bookstores. Most of these are merely textbooks that increase the reader's technical proficiency without inspiring them to attain new creative heights, or even challenge them to use their imaginations. Most are written from a computer literacy point of view and lack the insights gained from years of experience as a commercial photographer. Because of his background, Bryan Allen understands the technical aspects of photography and the demands of running a profitable business. Working with Photoshop is not just a job, but an adventure. His photographic techniques, as well as his Photoshop techniques, are based on the reality of the commercial world, where time is often critical and not always billable. Written from this perspective, his understanding of what it takes to get the job done along with his technical proficiency should be useful to everyone from Photoshop fledglings to advanced technicians. In fact, reading this book is like hiring several people—a business consultant to help you get your business started, a Photoshop tutor to teach you the most useful techniques, a pre-press specialist to help you get your images out in the right format, and a graphic designer to help you learn to how to turn your ideas into reality.

Bryan Allen pushes the creative envelope with Photoshop and he lets the reader of *Digital Wizardry* into his thought processes as he does it. But it isn't the only program he uses, and the author also explores other programs like MetaCreation's Bryce and Painter, that he's used to enhance his Photoshop experience and produce special effects outside the realm of Photoshop.

I could describe Bryan Allen as an Imaging Master and that would be praise enough for most, but he is also a conscientious and articulate author. Through this book, he has found a way to combine his photographic vision, his incredible imagination, and his technical proficiency into a manual that teaches more about the creative process than any other work on Photoshop. The beautiful photos and collages found in this book, combined with the step-by-step descriptions of the techniques he used to make them, prove that while technical proficiency is needed to master Photoshop, imagination and creativity are needed to become a Master. For that reason alone, *Digital Wizardry* is an exceptional book that I think should be a part of any Photoshop curriculum, and a reference to turn to when you need inspiration.

MICHAEL J. MCNAMARA
Technology Editor
Popular Photography Magazine

INTRODUCTION

In the early 1980s, the first quiet ripples of the digital shock wave reached the shores of the photographic community. Still working in New York as an assistant photographer at the time, I had only fearful thoughts of what the impact of this revolution would be on my new-found career. Mystery surrounded these electronic gadgets and their operators. Would they replace us? To me it seemed very much an "us against them" scenario. These early fears kept me dead set against the idea of going digital for some time.

Ten years later found me with my own business. At that time, I was using slide projectors as a means of doing in-camera collage work. I was projecting elements, sometimes with upwards of ten carousels, onto various surfaces and then photographing the result. It was a very tedious process. My friend, and partner at the time, suggested that sliding these elements around on a computer screen might be a smarter and simpler way to go about this. The realization that he might be right eventually overpowered my self-imposed avoidance of all things digital.

My first computer surprised me a lot. It was a Macintosh Quadra 700. I had no idea how much I was going to be captivated by this amazing new technology. Up until this time I had always been one who preferred low tech over high tech—antique furniture over new; sailboats over power boats; faded old jeans over slacks. This computer was the very antithesis of what I was. Yet I loved it.

There weren't many books on the subject of imaging and Photoshop at the time. Most of what I learned was from the program manual and from just playing around with the program and experimenting. I wished there was a book that was not too technical for a beginner like me and yet have loads of inspiring images to encourage me.

As time went by, several books did appear. Some beckoned with color covers but disappointed with only small, black-and-white images inside. Others covered every technical aspect of Photoshop so thoroughly that they competed with the unabridged dictionary for thickness. They weren't bad books; quite the contrary. They just weren't what I was looking for.

This book is intended to be the one that I never found. It is a colorful, inspirational how-to book, a long hard look under the hood of several professionally executed images. The descriptions of the images are not glossed over. If I made mistakes or encountered difficulties in their execution, you will read about it (and I hope learn from it).

Though many of the technical aspects of hardware, software, imaging, prepress, and the like are covered here, this book is *not* a technical manual. It is an idea book for creative people who want to either learn Photoshop or take their Photoshop skills to the next level. The beginner and intermediate digital imager will find plenty of very useful information without being buried by it.

I am still a Macintosh user. Though much of the information in this book applies easily to any platform, specific key commands, references to operating systems, and the like are particular to the Mac. I elected not to put the PC key-command equivalents in parentheses next to every Mac key command. If this bothers any PC users, stick around. You may yet have the last laugh if Apple continues down the slippery slope it seems to be on. Although I occasionally reference Photoshop 3.0, the book deals almost exclusively with version 4.0.

PART ONE

START WITH AN IDEA

You can produce the most technically brilliant shot, with every pixel massaged to perfection, but if the idea behind it is not good, the image will fall short every time. A portfolio of these images will show prospective clients your technical expertise, nothing more. A large percentage of what goes on in commercial imaging fits into this category of "grunt work," or execution, and I don't mean to belittle it. You can (and many do) make a career of it. This is not the kind of work we'll focus on here, though. This section will focus on the creation of stand-alone images that must convey a concept, dazzle, and be clever about it.

CHAPTER ONE

ANATOMY OF AN IDEA
CREATIVE BEGINNINGS

*"To swear off making mistakes is very easy.
All you have to do is swear off having ideas."*

LEO BURNETT

COMING UP with a solid idea for an image can be difficult, even if you are used to generating ideas on a regular basis. Some photographers I know claim to be the "non-idea" type. "Where do you come up with this stuff? I could never do that," they say as they look at my pictures. They often don't give themselves enough credit. Despite their claims, I've gone to them with the beginnings of an idea to get their input and suggestions. After the first few obligatory shrugs, they begin to warm to the process. By the end of fifteen minutes, the ideas are flowing freely.

If you count yourself among the inspirationally challenged, take heart. This chapter will look at a variety of methods for inspiring those recalcitrant ideas to the surface.

Those new to Photoshop sometimes have a hard time choosing a direction. Everything they do to their images seems fun and interesting. And although veteran imagers may wrinkle their noses at pictures that were distorted beyond recognition simply for distortion's sake, doing them can be a great way to learn the program. Once those newcomers have reached a reasonable level of proficiency, they will probably come back to the things that have always motivated them photographically. Stock shooters will find ways to produce shots they couldn't do before, and still-life people will do the same. Those who were already manipulating their images in the camera or in the darkroom will be in heaven and take right to it.

Step one, then, is to pick a direction or a look. Are you going to do collage work, altered realities, electronically enhanced straight photography? If you have some of each, putting them all in one book will not help you. If clients call because of collage pieces they saw, they are going to expect a book with more collages to confirm their initial choice. A mixed book will only confuse them. As good as the other work may be, it won't be what these people need to see at this particular moment. If you do different styles, as I do, advertise and show different books—separately.

THE SOURCE OF THE IDEA

Many assignments, plum or otherwise, come with the idea prehatched by the client. This is the situation many people thrive on and feel most comfortable with. You are pointed down a particular road and told to march, adding your own flourishes along the way.

The drawing below is from an art director who saw our Lightning Catchers shot (page 77) and wanted a variation that would show the empowerment of computers by his client's product, a software package. Our job was simply to execute the sketch and bring it to life.

The final sketch and the final image.

Just as often, though, you are handed only the nucleus of an idea, around which you are asked to flesh out an image. This can be a lot more challenging. The client is now asking you to solve a problem. "How do we illustrate this theme and not be deadly boring about it?"

Where do people get the ideas for their images? Ask them; the answers are as varied as they are fascinating. Most people I asked said their ideas were derivative of something else, as opposed to being completely self-generated. Interestingly, that "something else" was very rarely another photograph. Here are a number of methods that are used by the pros for coming up with ideas.

Think Tank Approach

Sitting down with two or more people is probably the most consistently powerful way of coming up with good ideas. It is also the best way, by far, to flesh out existing ones. I had a partner for a time and I can attest to this. My partner and I were more productive working this way than any other way. If we sat down with an assignment, it was only a matter of time before someone made a starting suggestion. If it was my partner, I would generally try to look at the idea from different perspectives. "How would that look if we made it a down shot?" for example. He would then take the idea, with its new perspective, and twist it some more. It may bounce back and forth several times in this early stage. This goes on for some time and many ideas will be tabled, rolled over in the mind, and written down. The details are not worried about at this stage. The ideas have to feel right first. The details will be fussed over later at the "fleshing out" stage. Someone working alone would need to be uncommonly focused and creative to match what two or more can do together.

Invariably, someone offers an idea or an addition to an idea that is intended only to make everyone laugh. Don't be too quick to ignore these comments. More than one good idea has come this way.

Where did that first idea—the one that gets the ball rolling—come from? The rest of the list that follows may help.

Literature

Literature is a medium that seems to exist almost exclusively to put imagery in your head. The trick is to realize it and to be receptive to any ideas you may get while reading an inspiring piece of work. Ideas may come while you are reading, or they may come some time later. My wife, also a photographer, gets a lot of her ideas from literature. She enjoys reading all kinds of books but finds that science fiction and old classics, like *The Hobbit*, are especially fertile materials for her. In addition, many books in these genres often have excellent, fantastic illustrations that you may also find inspiring.

My wife recently worked on an image that was inspired by a 1920s illustrated children's book that had been read to her as a child. There was a particular drawing that always made her mind wander off into a daydream. In the illustration, you look up at a monstrous tree with an elaborate, sun-dappled tree house perched high up in the branches. The tree is at the edge of a forest with a grassy field in the foreground. A solitary young boy is making his way across this field to his secret hideaway. The image captured the feelings of wonder and excitement that my wife felt when she was a kid building tree houses with her father. It was this emotional response to the image that intrigued her and that she then sought to duplicate in her image.

Movies

No matter what the area—outer space, underwater, or landscapes—there's a barrelful of movies for you to turn to for inspiration. Again, as with literature, the idea often doesn't come to you until some time after you initially see the inspiring footage. Some of the most incredible imagery is often found in movies that didn't quite "make it" commercially. *Brazil* comes to mind.

Museums

Museums are whole buildings devoted to the world's greatest creative thinkers. Here you'll find room after room filled with works from the masters of color, light, line, shape, texture, and composition. Museums are a paradise for idea seekers. The variety you'll find in the larger city museums make them worth the extra time and effort it may take to get there.

You'll want to record your thoughts as you're walking through the museum. Full-blown ideas for images could come to you either right there or later on, but you will see things that you will want to remember, such as two colors that work powerfully together, a border, thoughts on a portrait handling, the way light and shadow are used, and much more.

Music

This suggestion came from an artist I know who finds music very helpful in her work. Like literature, it also seems designed to put images in your mind's eye. If this artist friend is struggling in her attempts to put a good idea to an assigned theme or concept, she'll sit back and listen to her favorite instrumental music. I've tried this method and it works. It's tougher to let your mind wander while listening to lyrics, though, because the words do the work your imagination should be doing. I recommend sticking to instrumental pieces.

Memories

Memories of events or the emotions connected to the events are very strong resources for generating ideas. The firefly shot in Chapter Two was born of the fondness I have always had for the childhood memory of catching lightning bugs. I felt very sure about many of the aspects of that image because of the strength of the memory.

An unpleasant memory could also be the basis of a powerful shot. If you represent the emotion of the event in an arresting way, you have yourself a shot with real impact.

The list of ways to come up with ideas, of course, is endless. Inspired by a wide variety of sources, a great idea for a shot sometimes just leaps into your head. The problem is that it often leaps right back out before you have a chance to record it. Keep a notepad handy or at least get to your file of ideas before it vanishes. I wish I had back just half the ideas that seemed too good to forget.

Memories of past events can evoke strong images. My memories of chasing fireflies helped mold the image that this detail comes from.

Source Books

Going through the source books, such as the Black Book, is another good way to get you thinking. I like going through the books to see what other people are up to. It can be depressing if you let yourself get distracted by the realization that there are a lot of really talented photographers out there. If you get past this, though, you may see something that triggers an idea. It may even be just a piece of a shot. It may be the style. You may see a shot that attempts to illustrate a concept but you think of a much better way of doing it.

Let me be clear. I am not suggesting that anyone steal someone else's idea. If you are just starting out, though, you may find it useful to mimic a style that appeals to you. The process of imitating another work can lead to your coming up with your own unique style.

An interesting thing occasionally happens to me when I'm going through the books. If I'm turning the pages briskly enough, my eye will catch an image as it flashes past. Before I can even turn back the page to examine it more closely, I've got an image in my head. I'll be thinking, "Wow, was that a shot of X" and then I'll turn the page back to find it was nothing even close. The colors and shapes just made me think it was. But that image I had in my head before I turned the page back was an idea that I probably would not have come to without the stimulus of the picture flashing past. If you're thinking the guys in the white coats should arrive at any second to drag me away, I dare you to try it first.

When I first began as a photographer, I made the false assumption that all the shots in my portfolio had to look a certain way, that they had to fit someone else's criteria. The images I worked on were chosen because I thought that's what art directors wanted to see. The shots were somewhat sterile as a result. I shot things for myself that were much more interesting to me but I never showed them. Now I've come full circle. Commercial photography has moved much closer to fine art and that has given all photographers the chance to experiment more and be more daring with their ideas. Don't leave your most daring works out of your book.

FLESHING OUT THE IDEA

With your list of ideas in hand, the next step is to sit down with a sketch pad. If you are not especially good at drawing, you may find yourself spending more time staring at the blank page than you do sketching. Don't get hung up on the accuracy of the drawing. The trick is to commit any ideas worth pursuing to paper—quickly. Sketching the idea is a very important step. An idea that seemed terrific in your head, once physically down on paper, may turn out to need a lot more work, or you may decide it is not even worth pursuing. Conversely, a sketch may confirm that the idea is good, but that there are compositional problems still to be worked out.

If you get into the habit of working this way, do yourself a favor and start a file so that you can save all these sketches. Go back to this file once in a while and take a look. You'll likely see many ideas that you had written off and forgotten about. One or two that were good but didn't have that edge, that special twist that pushes them over the top, may interest you all over again. That missing ingredient that gave you such grief and eluded you just months ago may come easily now.

GETTING IT RIGHT

These sketches show the evolution of an idea from start to finish. We had to illustrate the breadth of the trademark names in a particular division of Warner Lambert for its annual report. There were four other shots in the series. Since we had seen and liked several illustrations done as analogies, we decided to work the ideas around a photo analogy or altered-reality format. The clients stressed that they wanted the image to show how the products and the trade names have "elevated" the company.

My partner got the ball rolling with an idea that involved "little executives" standing on top of tall stone columns, hauling the trade names up with a rope. I liked this first idea. It was visually interesting and kind of gave "shape" to the theme. It helped me get started with variations of my own. We each added a few more ideas and then two sketches were done.

We liked the results, so far, but knew that we couldn't present just one idea for each theme. Coming up with ideas using the "little execs" was proving to be easy, but we couldn't use them in all five images. We decided to try to come up with "exec-free" versions for each of the five pictures. This put us back to square one with the trade name shot.

We struggled a bit with this new direction. "How can we show a bunch of names, without people interacting, and still make it exciting?" we asked ourselves. We decided to have the names appear to be carved in stone on some sort of plaque or tablet and then just "try on" different backgrounds until something seemed right. We started with the plaque supported by columns and surrounded by water and a rocky coastline. Exquisite, late-afternoon sunlight would fill out the picture. We liked this start. We had been wanting to use an ocean landscape for some time.

The idea still seemed weak, and though we continued to work it, it never quite got there. The next thought found the plaque up in the mountains. But why put a stone plaque on a stone mountain? Why not just carve the names into the mountainside like a Mount Rushmore of trade names? This sounded interesting but it was missing something. A normal-size young executive was added, hanging from a rope with chisel in his hand. Initially the perspective was looking slightly up with a wide lens, but it changed to looking slightly down so that the viewer could see all the way to the valley floor. Golden sunset light was imagined in this scene and that was it. We had another good version to show the clients.

The best two or three ideas were drawn in a much more finished and presentable way and colored in. Smaller details were also discussed and worked out. Should the young executive wear corporate clothes or climbing gear? What should we see down in the valley?

A few technical questions had to be answered before the clients could see the drawings. "How do we get the carved letters convincingly into the mountain?" I'd hate to have to tell the clients that I couldn't execute my own idea. The drawings were also passed around to others for additional comments, including the designers at the design shop who were putting the annual together. This is a very valuable step. Everyone sees things a little differently and it's helpful to hear what they have to say. Good suggestions often come from people seeing the idea for the first time. They almost always have a thought on a missing detail, a compositional problem, or another problem that those of us too close to the project have become blind to.

Even after everyone signs off on the drawing, changes and refinements are likely to take place. A low-resolution computer "sketch," using as many real elements as possible, will usually suggest a few of these refinements.

This first direction, with little executives, was pleasing to us but the clients decided we should explore other directions.

The second direction gave us an excuse to use the ocean, but the idea was weak and would have relied too heavily on the effects and the execution for its strength.

The final sketch gave us a nice combination of drama and lighting while avoiding the little people that were already in one of the other shots in the series.

JET LIGHTER
OVERCOMING OBSTACLES

I T'S DIFFICULT TO RECALL all the details and the problems encountered while producing an image when you sit down to write about it months later. Obstacles and difficulties that seemed so important at the time fade away in memory and new challenges occupy your professional energies.

I have described here the creation of an image as a work in progress. I have chosen this image because it was being done for the portfolio. As such, it was able to evolve and change more than an image that had constraints imposed on it by a client. Hopefully, revealing problems or surprises that I failed to anticipate will help you a little and not tarnish my reputation too much.

THE IDEA
I had an idea for an image involving a jet. There were low-level aerial shots over water, boats, the jet itself, and all sorts of things going on. The mounting complexity of the shot bothered me, but I liked it enough to push on. I spent a considerable amount of time trying mentally to sort out the long list of technical and logistical chal-

The mechanic at McGuire Air Force Base was shot from the waist up. This ended up being problematic.

lenges. On the top of that list was getting a trail of fire and smoke to come from the jet's afterburners. I figured some sort of blowtorch, cranked up really high, might be a good place to start. It was at this point that I remembered how a friend of mine lit his cigarettes with a small, trigger-operated propane torch. An idea for a much simpler shot with just as much impact followed soon after.

My brother, who is in the Air Force and stationed not too far away, told me about a fighter jet on static display that I could photograph to my heart's content. I would also be allowed to put a strobe light in the "tailpipe." In addition, there was an interesting-looking mechanic on the base who was willing to be in the shot. I felt things were working out well.

THE FIRST SHOOT
The mechanic worked out perfectly. He looked great and the more people gathered around to watch him, the more animated he became. I originally wanted to shoot him out by the jet, but that was not possible. Instead, the lights were set up in the hangar he works in. The entire west wall of the hangar was glass and I was able to use the natural light to augment the strobes.

The jet was there, as promised. It was an F-4. The problem was that the afterburner port was set back under the tail by about 8 feet. I had asked my brother several questions about the jet. "Are there afterburner ports on this jet?" "Are they the right height?" "Is the port covered or can I put a strobe inside?" My big mistake was assuming that the port would be all the way at the back of the plane. Wrong!

I lit and then shot the port anyway, figuring I could strip it into a picture of another jet or even a model jet. Since finding another plane would be difficult at this point, I got a model of an F-16, which had the port where I wanted it. (These things were decidedly easy to put together because all that was needed was the tail.) Using the model

As a result of not asking enough preliminary questions, I arrived at the base to find a jet that was not quite what I expected.

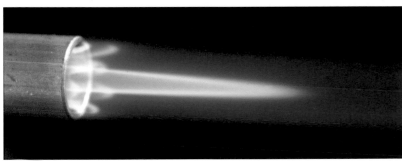

In its raw form, this shot of the propane torch flame looks very crude. By copying and pasting the long portion of the flame, enlarging it substantially, and colorizing it to a more yellow-orange hue, the flame turned out to be quite workable.

was an acceptable solution because I shot at dusk, used Motion Blur, and then tacked the real afterburner back on afterward.

PAYING ATTENTION TO DETAIL

Next, I photographed the flame of a propane torch. I thought with some work it would look okay. The Air Force guys told me that the real thing looked like concentric cones of flame, so I had that imagery to go on when I put the torch flame into the shot. To get the concentric flames I just made a duplicate layer, enlarged it a few hundred percent, and laid it directly over the first shot.

I did see a potential problem with this torch flame, though. It had a very transparent quality. I originally had envisioned a more opaque flame that would basically cover the lower half of the model. Since he was only photographed from the

waist up, I either had to shoot a different flame or give him some legs. I rather liked the transparent look of the flame so I opted to give the mechanic some legs. Going all the way back to the base to reshoot the mechanic was not practical so I shot someone else in the studio This was fairly straightforward since I had measured the camera height and angle to ensure consistency among the major elements.

The model of the jet was shot outside, in open shade, just before sunset. Film from a photo of the real jet helped me line up the initial angle, although I shot a bunch of angles around this starting point anyway. The lens that was used on the mechanic and the real jet was used here as well.

I thought about using a model for the carrier as well, but I was nervous enough about using a model for so large an element as the jet. Besides,

Rather than attempt to re-create the diffuse light of dawn in the studio, I took the model plane outside and photographed it in open shade.

The model jet has been darkened down considerably here and the afterburner from the real jet has been added.

By photographing someone in the studio from the same camera height and angle, I was able to give the mechanic his legs back.

the real thing was only an hour away at the U.S.S. *Intrepid*, an air and space museum in New York City. I went on an overcast day and shot the deck and the superstructure. Once placed into the image it could be darkened down to get the dusk effect I wanted.

Here are the two pieces of film that I used of the carrier. I couldn't get far enough away from the superstructure because of some static displays and because the *Intrepid* is small by today's standards. I could have scaled the superstructure down, but I liked the runway lines better on the second shot anyway. I put the superstructure on top of this deck and then reduced it. This gave me the expansive feel I was after.

The last major element to deal with was the sky. I used a shot of sea and sky that I found in my files. It had the atmospheric qualities that suggested dusk and, in addition, allowed me to place the image in the ocean.

PUTTING IT ALL TOGETHER

It's time to see what happened when all the elements were put together. This was the fun part. Many days were spent pulling elements together, scanning, cutting paths, and handling details that are, by themselves, not very interesting. In the span of just a few minutes, though, the changes came rapidly and the image in my mind started to emerge on the screen.

This was the first go around. Once you've seen the final (page 16), the changes that were needed here will seem obvious. I now see many things that I didn't notice then. The jet and the carrier both needed to be darkened quite a bit. I wanted some lights on both of them to add interest and to heighten the feeling of it being dusk. The mechanic was supposed to be holding marshaling lights, but since I didn't have them the day of the shoot, I had him hold flashlights. His hands were at least in the right gesture. All I had to do was paint on the tops.

The biggest problem was that because the cigarette was too small it didn't read well. If the cigarette isn't a quick read, the whole shot is a bust. Cropping helped. The fact that less of the jet showed didn't hurt the image. I liked the background the way it was, however. I decided to put off making a decision on this one while I dealt with some of the other issues.

The Motion Blur I used for the jet worked very nicely. The lighter areas were generously feathered after being acquired with Color Range. These areas were then darkened down with Curves.

The same treatment, with an extra twist, was given to the deck. After the selection was made and feathered, it was saved as an Alpha Channel and deselected. Quick Mask was then used with the Gradient tool set to Linear to produce a soft, top to bottom, gradated selection. The Alpha Channel was then opened using the Intersect command. The result was a selection that was weighted to the foreground. (See the Quick Mask and Alpha Channels section, page 18.)

An overcast day was just what I wanted for shooting the deck of the Intrepid (above left). A static display forced me to get closer to the superstructure than I wanted, so I also shot a piece of deck (above right) because of the increased width I was able to get. The superstructure was eventually pasted here for a more expansive look.

The first look at the assembled elements revealed several challenges to be overcome.

The detail below shows the results of using the Gradient tool to fill the door on the right with two tones of yellow.

The lights in the deck were made with the Paintbrush. The shape of the brush itself was changed to a horizontal oval. The Airbrush, set to about 10 percent opacity, was used to paint in the glow with a lighter version of the same color. The red lights were done with the Airbrush only. An extra dab of the light red was placed in the center.

The orange tops of the marshaling lights were painted in next. I used the Dodge tool on the long edges to give them some shape. One of the lights was copied into a separate file, given a Spin Radial Blur, and brought back to the image. After being placed, it was copied, rotated, and put over the second light.

Be careful about overusing the Dodge and Burn tools. The Dodge tool lightens things by adding white. The Burn tool adds black. With critical areas, take the trouble to make a selection and then use something like Curves.

MAKING ADJUSTMENTS

I decided, finally, to enlarge the two front elements and to leave the background alone, rather than cropping in. Although it enhanced the expansive feel of the carrier, it still didn't solve the cigarette problem. I decided to go with a cigar.

I also decided to trade in the gray ocean and sky background for a more colorful sunrise shot. There was already so much blue in the shot, I thought the red would liven up the image and play off the reds in the foreground.

The challenge here was to make the appropriate areas of the carrier and the jet look like they are being bathed in red light. I did this by making selections with Color Range, feathering them to 10 pixels, and then shifting the color with a combination of Selective Color and Curves.

I put the cigar in and it seemed to work. The larger size really helped. When the cigar was shot, a propane torch was positioned near the end of it so as to push a flame off to one side. The end of the cigar didn't glow as brightly as I had hoped so it was goosed up in Photoshop. Curves and Color Balance did the trick.

Two shots, the cigar and a flame for its end, were stored on one file in the Elements folder (above left). Bits of wood were burned to capture flames for the brim of the hat (above right).

The image was looking very monochromatic so a little color was added. Putting a slice of the shot here at left into the background was easy. Making the rest of the image look as though the sky was red all along was much more challenging.

The last touches were the flames and sparks flying off the brim of the hat. I was going to burn an actual hat, but after looking at the film of the mechanic, I decided to use flames taken from a burning piece of wood instead. The propane torch was placed next to the wood and a hairdryer was held near to help the sparks fly.

Glowing embers scanned from this film were placed along the edge of the hat's brim and the flames and sparks were placed afterward. The fly-ing sparks were weak and I found it necessary to strengthen them with the Paintbrush and Airbrush.

Would images like this one be as challenging and as much fun if they always went smoothly? Tough call. They would certainly get done faster. Yet coming up against an obstacle and then negotiating a way past it is very satisfying. When it comes right down to it, any job without prob-lem solving is ultimately a boring one (and one with lower pay as well).

The final image shows dramatic improvement over the initial assembly.

START WITH AN IDEA

COLOR TO GRAY TO COLOR
CREATING UNIQUE EFFECTS

HERE IS AN INTERESTING technique to try. You may not use it every day but it is a good one for your bag of tricks, all the same. What you are going to do is convert a color image to Bitmap mode, convert it back to RGB (Red, Green, Blue), and then add color to it. It will have a more unique look than a colorized gray scale image or a duotone.

You can start with an image in layers, but you will be asked to merge them along the way. Strong graphic shapes work better than many fussy details. The image can be color or black and white. For this example I'm starting with a color image.

First, make the image gray scale if it isn't already. Go up to Image in the menu bar, down to Mode, and over to Gray scale. Hit OK. Once that is done, go right back up to the same place but this time choose Bitmap. A dialog box will come up. Of the choices that are offered here, take Diffusion Dither. The output number should be such that you have around 1000 to 1500 pixels on the long side of the image. Hit OK again. Now go up and switch the mode, this time back to Gray scale. You will be asked about the Size Ratio. Leave it at 1. Make one last mode switch from Gray scale to RGB.

Since the physical resolution of your monitor is only about 72 dpi (dots per inch), you will probably have to zoom in a bit to see the image more clearly. Going down to Actual Pixels under View in the menu will also work.

Now for the fun part. The image is made up of only black-and-white pixels. Open Color Range, and at the top of the palette that comes up, choose Shadows from the Select menu. Hit OK. All the black pixels are selected. Don't feather the selection. Do hit Command-H to hide that army of marching ants, though. Pick two dark colors in the Toolbox for the foreground and background colors. With the Gradient tool, make a blend of the two colors across the image. Here I'm using a Linear Blend but it could just as easily be a Radial Blend. Select Inverse from the Select column, hide the edges again with Command H, and pick two new, lighter colors for the highlights. Do another Gradient Blend. After the second blend, leave the selection alone and start playing with things like Curves, Inverse, Gaussian Blur, and Hue Saturation.

Two different color gradients have been applied to this Bitmapped-turned-RGB file.

A close-up of the image shows off the Bitmapped pattern.

ALPHA CHANNELS
SAVING COMPLEX SELECTIONS

A SELECTION MADE with the Lasso can be saved as a path (see the section on Paths in Chapter Four, page 92). If the selection was made using a feathered Lasso, you can still save it as a path as long as you remember to feather it again when you convert it back to a selection. In this situation, I would make myself a note right in the name of the path; "Path1-feather to 15," for example.

What do you do with a complicated selection like one made with Color Range? You could make a path out of it, but it would never be quite the same again, even with feathering. Color Range selections often involve pixels that are partially selected mingled with fully selected ones.

These selections can be saved as an Alpha Channel. Any time there is a selection on the screen, the Save Selection command will be highlighted and ready for use at the bottom of the Select column in the menu.

Once the selection is saved as an Alpha Channel, it can be loaded at any time with the Load Selection command, also at the bottom of the

Select column. You can use any of the other selection tools to add to or to subtract from the selection. If this "updated" selection makes the original obsolete, go to the Save Selection dialog box, choose the old Alpha Channel name, and check the Replace Channel radio button to save over the original.

You can also go to the Channels palette and modify it. When you click once on the Alpha Channel that needs attention, the image channels are turned off leaving only the Alpha Channel or mask in all its black-and-white glory. The white area represents the selection and the black area is masked from view. You may have noticed that the foreground and background colors also become black and white when the channel was activated. If you now take one of the paint tools and paint over any of the white areas with black, the mask and its resulting selection would be smaller. Painting in, or erasing to white any of the black areas makes it larger. Using any shade of gray results in partially selected pixels the next time the channel is converted back to a selection. Soft brushes result in feathered selections and

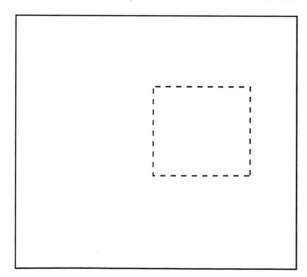

A simple selection gets saved as an Alpha Channel by using the Save Selection command in the Select menu column.

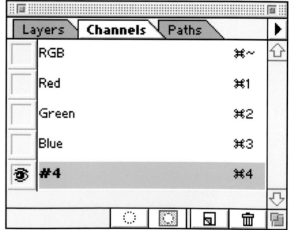

To edit the channel, click once on the channel name.

hard-edged brushes result in sharper selections. Try it. You can even apply effects and filters to all or part of the channel to alter it.

Another way to create a new channel is to use the Paste Into command while a selection is on the screen. The element you pasted is all there but only the portion within the selection area is visible. The rest is hidden by a Layer Mask. Why not delete the unseen portion of the element? Would you glue your furniture to the floor? You might want to go back and move it. If the element you want to partially hide is already on the screen, make a selection that describes what portion of the element you wish to hide or reveal. Go up to the Layer column and down to Add Layer Mask. Among the choices will be Hide Selection and Reveal Selection. A layer can have only one Layer Mask at a time.

If you have several Alpha Channels and are using them regularly, I recommend giving them names that describe what they are masking. To change the name, double click the Alpha Channel name in the Channels palette, just as you would when changing a layer name.

Unlike paths, Alpha Channels can take up a fair amount of memory. If you save the file in the Photoshop format, however, the Alpha Channel information is compressed and therefore won't use as much memory.

When you collapse the layers in your image and save a separate version to disk, you may want to throw away the channels and paths. Conversely, if you are trying to save a file to disk and you keep getting "Disk is Full" messages, the disk is empty, and the Image Size window says it should fit, you probably have an Alpha Channel that you forgot to get rid of.

A complex selection may take several steps and require that the first steps are saved as an Alpha Channel. In the example on pages 20–21, I wanted to select the deeper blues in the water and make them darker with Curves. But I also wanted the effect of Curves to be progressively stronger toward the foreground.

The Color Range selection in the first image is feathered to 3 pixels and then saved as an Alpha Channel. After selecting None, Quick Mask is activated by hitting the Q key. The Gradient tool is used to make a linear blend from black to white. When the Q key is tapped again, a smoothly gradated selection that encompasses the entire image will result. But I didn't want to affect the entire image, just the areas grabbed in

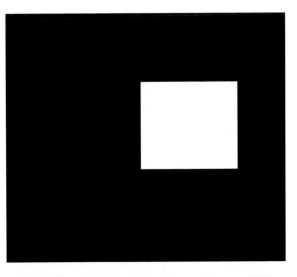

The image on the screen becomes the channel itself. Painting or erasing to white or black makes the channel larger or smaller.

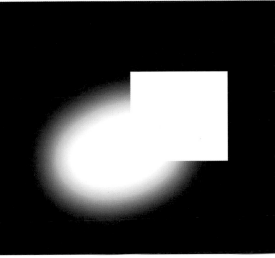

An eraser with a soft brush was used to expand the channel.

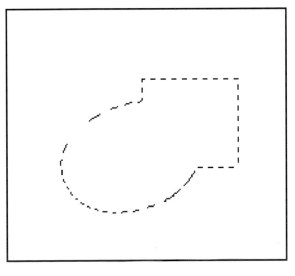

The new selection that loads from the channel has a hard edge along the original square and a soft edge along the new area.

the first selection. So that first Alpha Channel is opened with the Load Selection command, found at the bottom of the Select menu.

At the bottom of the Load Selection palette there is a radio button to choose Intersect with Selection. When you hit OK, the intersection of the two selections is all that remains. When I then apply any change to the selection, it will be progressively stronger toward the side I want it to be, the bottom in this case. Notice how I have filled it with white so that the effect shows up better.

If you are trying to save a file and the mode you want, such as JPEG, is grayed out, there are still layers that need to be merged or Alpha Channels that need to be deleted. Paths won't cause the same problem, but for files being output, I would throw these away as well.

Arriving at complex selections takes a few steps. Step one in this case involved making a Color Range selection and saving it as an Alpha Channel.

The second step was to make a graduated selection with Quick Mask and save it as an Alpha Channel as well.

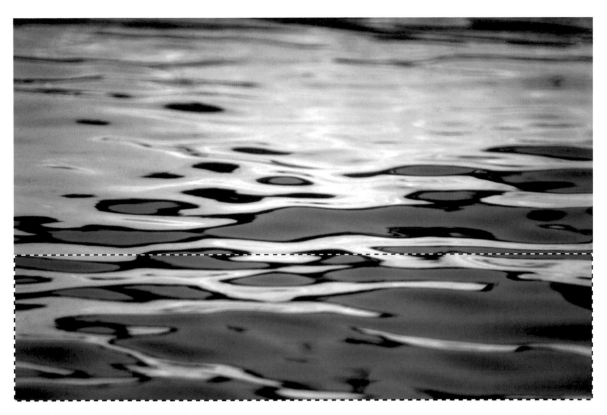

The appearance of the selection that results from using the Blend tool with Quick Mask belies its heavily feathered qualities. Making a selection like this with the Lasso would be difficult if not impossible.

I have filled the selection with white so that the qualities of the compound selection show up better.

CHAPTER TWO

GARBAGE IN, GARBAGE OUT
MASTERING QUALITY CONTROL

"Most people don't recognize opportunity when they see it because it is usually dressed in overalls and looks a lot like work."

THOMAS EDISON

SOME YEARS AGO I built a small boat. She turned out okay. The plans had called for southern white cedar but pine was easier to come by and was much cheaper, too. Instead of sitka spruce for the mast I just used a cut down 4 x 4 bought at the lumberyard. Seven coats of varnish seemed excessive; it looked so good after only three. Stainless steel became galvanized. "Good enough" became the phrase of the day.

I proudly brought my boat to the beach, glistening under layers of new white paint and looking like a million bucks. The old-timers said, "You did a good job with the materials you had, kid." I puffed up with pride, not recognizing the gentle chiding that was being administered. If you had asked those guys what was wrong with the boat exactly, they might have been hard pressed to say, but they knew. They just knew. Well, she sailed nicely at first but fell apart after a short while. I learned an expensive lesson with that project.

Of course, I had to relearn the lesson when I got into photography, and learn it again when I got into computers. I guess I'm just a slow learner. Building an electronic image may be worlds apart from building a boat, but a few basic rules apply to both. Take a good idea, combine it with high-quality materials and craftsmanship, and you will have a product that sells every time. Remember, though, that quality costs. Luckily for us imagers, it costs largely in the form of time and effort. It is the quality of the elements that make up our electronic images that I will address in this chapter.

QUALITY COUNTS

While the majority of commercial photographs are set up and taken in only a few hours, complex computer-generated images can take days and even weeks. The temptation to cut corners or to force mediocre elements to work by jazzing them up in the computer becomes a strong one. Why photograph a dollar bill for that business collage when you've already got a perfectly workable one in your files? Even if you choose to shoot it, who's going to know if you just plop it down in a patch of sunlight instead of putting up a set and shooting Polaroids? Why take models out on location when you can shoot them in your studio and strip them into your shot later? Isn't this the point of having the computer in the first place? Why buy a larger scanner with better

resolution and dynamic range when your current scanner is working fine? Why should you build three-dimensional letters just to photograph them? Why not render them in a three-dimensional program and hope that they blend with the photographed elements? Why not indeed?

Cutting Corners

The scary part about cutting corners is that you can actually get away with it every once in a while. This is just enough to tempt you to try it again. Don't. If your goal is to produce top-shelf images that get you noticed and keep the phones ringing, you have to treat every last detail as if it were the most important one.

Everyone begins an image with high expectations. It's in the execution where things start to fall short, very often when decisions about element creation are being made. When you sit down to assemble your shot and you have nothing but gorgeous, technically excellent elements to work with, your job will be a lot easier. As with most commercial photo shoots, preparation is nine-tenths of the work.

Clearly there will be times when you have neither the time nor the budget to produce shots that live up to your highest standards. If herculean efforts were applied to every single shot that came through your shop, your eyes would turn square long before you got to the important ones. Save the corner cutting for the low-budget, we-need-it-yesterday images that won't make it to the portfolio. Perhaps you are working on an image for your portfolio or on a project whose budget is not good, but the images would really help your portfolio. These are the shots that warrant those extra hours. Put in the time on these and you won't be sorry.

MAKING YOUR IDEA COME TO LIFE

The photo on the next page is an example of an image whose various elements were given careful consideration to ensure success. The two kids are catching lightning bugs and discovering they've caught more than they bargained for. I wanted the shot to do more than just tell this story though. Most of us can recall the childhood experience of catching fireflies in the early summer. I really wanted the feel of the place and the light to evoke those memories.

The light, especially, had to be just right—that soft, bluish, last light of day that seems to slowly filter straight down like dew, leaving any areas

near or under trees and shrubs dark and feature- less. I was determined to do whatever was nec- essary to capture this feel. It was a bit like doing a painting. For this reason, the two kids were photographed outdoors. Initially I was really tempted to shoot them in the studio and, with careful lighting, it might have worked. There is one compact light source and much of the boys are in shadow. But imitating outdoor light in the studio is a tough thing to do. You've all seen the shots in ads or in the source books; the studio shots that are supposed to look like they were shot at the beach or in the woods. If it was done well, you probably spent a lot of time looking for clues as to how the photographer got as close as he or she did. Still, you knew it was faked. Like the old- timers and the boat, you just knew.

The fireflies posed another prob- lem. Circumstances dictated that we complete this shot by May, so live lightning bugs were not yet out in New Jersey. I spent a considerable amount of time surfing the net for a place where they might already be out but had no luck. I then consid- ered using dead ones obtained from a zoological collection. Dead ones cooperate much better. I could have posed them just so and made their wings look as if they were flapping like mad in Photoshop. Dead ones are always available for reshoots and never go out of sea- son. But this idea was discarded fairly quickly. The legs on dead bugs always look, well, dead.

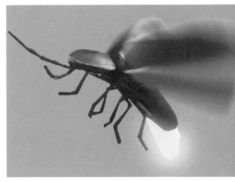

Making a model of a firefly took less time than looking for a real one. It was much more cooperative than a live one would have been. After blurring the wings and adding some light, the model became a convincing firefly.

The final solution was building a clay model of a firefly. This worked very well. I could have saved myself a lot of trouble had I thought of it sooner. In Photoshop, the flapping wings were made with the help of the Radial Blur filter set to Spin mode. Although the model bug's light was painted a bright color, it was selected and bright- ened with Curves. A separate glow layer for the phosphorescent effect of the bug's light was added. On this layer, the Airbrush, set to 12 per- cent opacity, sprayed a thin layer of very light green color.

A lot of energy went into capturing the light and the feel of a summer night.

For this particular glow, the molecule was blurred twice—once heavily and once less so. Each blur began as a separate layer.

MAKING AN OBJECT GLOW

To make an object glow, start by creating a duplicate of the target layer. This new layer will form just above the original. Make the original layer the active layer again and apply a strong Gaussian Blur. Open the Curves palette and brighten the blurred layer by about 30 percent. Now reduce the opacity of the unblurred, duplicate layer to about 65 percent. The object will seem to be generating its own light thanks to the brightened and blurred layer showing through. Pull down the opacity and/or brighten the blurred layer further for a stronger effect.

Photographing an element that will ultimately have quite a bit of contrast, such as an object in late-day sun, requires some extra attention. Be sure to fill the shadow side with enough diffuse light so that not only does the film have good shadow detail, but the resulting scan does as well. Most desktop scanners don't handle deep shadows very well. If you've ever tried to scan a chrome with poor shadow detail and then make it look like something, you know exactly what I'm talking about. You might even find yourself scanning a contrasty image twice, once for the shadows and once again for the highlights, and then combining the two in Photoshop.

Filling the shadows results in chromes that look a bit more opened up than you would care for in a stand-alone image, but you will be darkening down these shadows in the computer. The result will be rich detail in your shadows if you need it and the option to remove it if you don't. Either way, it's nice to have options.

The two pictures of the man in the lab coat on the facing page illustrate the point. The first picture is the original image. The shadow side of the model is filled, almost too much. The second image is a detail of the final. Here, the shadows glow with detail and give a richer look than shadows made up only of black.

Photographing elements on white seamless often proves to be a time saver. One or two clicks of the Magic Wand on the white area, select Inverse, and bang, you've got your selection. It sure beats using the Pen tool (see Paths, Chapter Four). If the element is destined for a darker background, however, the white seamless will not prove to be much of a time saver. Too much white will be selected. It can often be fixed, but it is so much easier and smarter to have the model stand on a surface similar in value to that of the final image. This holds true for elements that will end up on a brightly colored ground as well.

When shooting items for a collage, try placing them on textured and/or colored backgrounds and bringing some of that background along

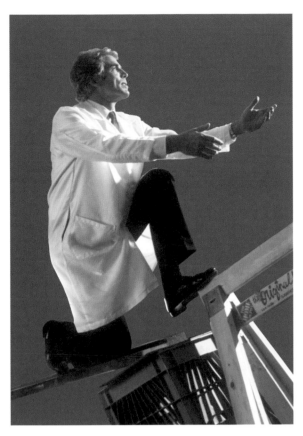

Although I knew the shadow side was going to end up fairly rich in the final image, it was given enough light to allow good detail even after the heavy darkening (left). In the detail of the final image (right) you see the darkened shadow side that had been filled so strongly. (Notice, also, that I've added a mustache, at the request of the clients, to give the character more personality.) The entire final image can be seen on pages 2 and 3.

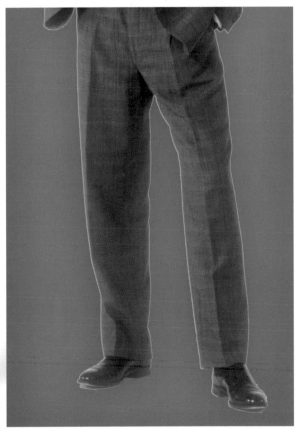

Shooting on white for easy silouetting isn't the right answer for elements headed for a dark background. Not only does too much white come along at the edge of the selection, but the white may also creep further into the element as a soft halo.

When assembling elements for a collage, shooting them on varied and interesting backgrounds will give you options later.

In the image below, the rusty metal behind the hand was shot separately and used for the background of the final. This hand was shot against the same background even though it was selected off and placed into the final. Had I shot against white or some other surface, I would have had to deal with the color difference at the motion-blurred edges.

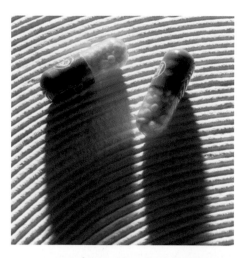

with the element into the shot. Use a feathered lasso set at, say, 30 pixels. This can often add quite a bit of depth and interest to an otherwise dull grouping. You may end up clipping away much of this texture later, but again, taking the extra time with the element early will give you choices later.

GOING FROM ORDINARY TO EXTRAORDINARY

"A lesson earned is better than a lesson learned if it don't come too dear," goes the old Maine saying. I've "earned" a few big lessons with bad scans. I still get chills remembering the trouble they have caused me. There was a major retouching job on a group executive portrait for an annual report. The client wanted a head from this frame, a smile from that frame, eyes from another, reduced wrinkles on this guy, twenty pounds off of that guy. The results of harsh top lighting had to be dealt with. "Can you make the CEO sit up straighter?" they asked. The walls and carpet both got new colors. This was a total repair job, but they were paying well and after more hours than I'd care to admit, the thing actually came together.

I was feeling good until the first match print came back. "There's a problem." The dreaded words drifted over the phone line. "The color isn't right and the shadow areas have an odd chalky quality to them." "Hey, no problem," I said feeling invincible with my mighty computer. "I'll just tweak the color and adjust the shadows until we get it right." Well, I tweaked and adjusted, output film and proofs, and then kept right on tweaking and adjusting, but the file refused to be brought to its knees.

The skin tones kept coming out kind of bronzy. I blamed the guys at the separation house. They said the problem was caused by bad scans. "Can't be. These were done on a Kodak Pro CD machine."

My contact at the separation house had me come in so he could explain exactly what was going on and why. It was a humbling experience; he was right. They *were* bad scans. The Kodak scanner is a good machine, but it turned out that the guys that were running it had just gotten it. There were apparently a few bugs in their system. I ended up having to re-scan everything and start over. It's funny how some things can be fairly enjoyable the first time around but feel like six hours in a dentist's chair the next time.

Had I been better familiarized with the Information palette, I might have caught the problem myself. I would have seen that the pixels did not receive all the depth they should have in the scanning process.

Running the cursor over the image with the Information palette open reveals a lot of data about the image. The information in the window reflects the color information for the pixel under the cursor. The pixels in those bad scans that looked black on the screen and were supposed to print black would have told another story in the Info palette had I known to look. I do now.

For a pixel to print black, the numbers that represent C, M, Y, and K should total at least 260 to 300. The total in the scans was only 210. (To see Total Ink as one of the readouts in the Info window, go to Palette Options by clicking on the arrow in the upper right of the palette.)

If you are getting your scans from an outside source, you would do well to check them for proper color depth and D-max before you invest too much time. Zoom in close and look for dust specks as well. A few are acceptable, but if your scan looks like a negative of the Milky Way, then someone didn't bother to clean off your film before scanning it. I had such a dust problem from one service bureau that I made them open the files before I accepted them. They eventually got smart and cleaned up their act, but so did I. I bought my own scanner. Now I charge for scans instead of paying for them.

At right is a detail from a scan made with an older Microtek desktop scanner. Next to it is the same section scanned with a newer desktop scanner made by Polaroid. Notice the noise and color breaks in the first scan. The Histograms also have a story to tell.

The color breaks in the scan show up as voids in the Histogram. (See Chapter Five for more information on scanners.)

Just getting to a point where you can begin to use electronic imaging in your work will take quite an investment in time and money. You will have purchased a powerful computer, a decent-sized monitor, a Zip drive or equivalent, perhaps a scanner. You have come much too far to get lazy about how you create and assemble your elements. I promise you, your extra efforts will be richly rewarded.

The number in the upper left is the sum of the four inks to the right. Total ink is one way of judging the quality of the blacks. The exclamation point next to the numbers tell me that the sampled pixel is out of CMYK Gamut.

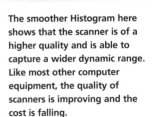

The choppy Histogram of this detail confirms what your eyes can already see. There are color breaks and noise in the shadow areas. When you demo a scanner, bring the test files back with you and look for those types of problems.

The smoother Histogram here shows that the scanner is of a higher quality and is able to capture a wider dynamic range. Like most other computer equipment, the quality of scanners is improving and the cost is falling.

SIMPLE NUDE
EXPERIMENTING WITH COLOR TOOLS

HUMANS ARE FUNNY CREATURES. Something will happen and we say to ourselves, "Gee, I sure learned a lesson there." A month goes by and the same set of circumstances comes along, this time disguised as something a little different, and we have to "learn" the same lesson all over again.

It was only after my mouse button stuck that I remembered a little maxim I promised myself I would try to live by. "Whenever you have any kind of dialog box or palette open, push the settings way beyond what is needed, just to see what happens." Nine times out of ten it wrecks the image. Once in a while, though, something really interesting happens. (I can practically hear the groans of the prepress people.) You may not even use this on the shot you're working on now, but it may inspire an idea for the future.

This image is one that I thought might benefit from being brought into Painter and manipulated there. I was getting it ready, using Selective Color to tweak the blacks when all of a sudden, the mouse button stuck and there were no blacks. The slider got taken all the way down to minus

This is the original image. While getting the image prepped to be imported into Painter, I stumbled on to an interesting technique. The image never did make it to Painter.

100 percent. What an unusual effect! I decided to continue playing with Selective Color and see where I ended up. (See Selective Color on page 42.) I never did make it to Painter.

With Absolute chosen at the bottom of the Selective Color palette, here are the moves that got the ball rolling. In the reds and yellows, cyan was pulled down 20 percent. In the blacks, black was pulled down all the way to minus 100 percent. In the neutrals, black was pumped up 50 percent and cyan was brought down 20 percent. The result was the image shown here.

The light gray areas fairly begged for some color. Color Range was used to make the selection. With the shift key held down, several samplings were taken in order to get all the various grays.

Portions of the highlights in the back and heel were also selected and needed to be deselected with the Lasso. The final selection was feathered by 4 pixels and then the Colorize command in the Hue/Saturation palette was used to generate the blue. I next wanted to blur some parts of the figure to give the image more depth and interest. I decided to achieve this by blurring the entire shot first and then pasting a clean copy of the figure back in and erasing away areas to reveal the blur. With the colorizing selection still on the screen, the Inverse command was used and the resulting selection copied. After selecting None, the entire image was given a Gaussian Blur to a radius of about 35 (file size: 4 x 5 inches x 600 dpi). Even when you don't think that a fresh copy will need

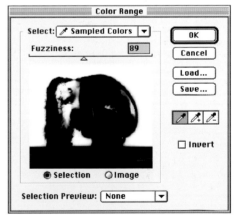

This is the result of the blacks being taken down to zero in Selective Color. The reds and yellows were also cleaned up by having some cyan pulled out.

The Color Range window shows that a few areas in the figure will need to be deselected.

With Selective Color, the blacks were taken out completely.

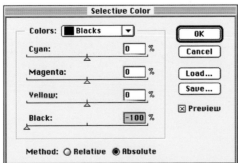

to be pasted in, it's a good idea to copy the critical areas first before making wholesale changes.

The clean copy of the figure was pasted back onto the blurred image. The opacity of this new layer was pulled down to 50 percent, giving the image a shimmering glow. With a large, soft Eraser in Paintbrush mode and set to 50 percent opacity, I took away a lot of the less important information. This included the floor, feet, and some of the strong line along the back.

I liked a lot of what I was doing to this layer but I got a little carried away in some areas. Too much of the figure got erased. Rather than throwing it away and starting over, I decided to paste another copy of the figure directly on top of the first layer. This second layer was set to an opacity of 30 percent. With that same Eraser now set to 80 percent opacity, I removed nearly everything but the detail that needed to be put back in.

Color Range was used to select the gray background prior to its being colorized a deep blue.

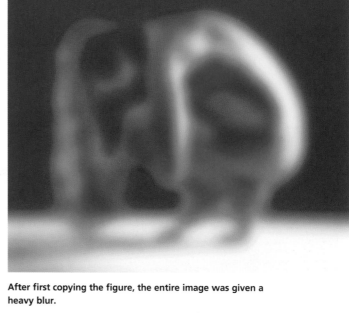

After first copying the figure, the entire image was given a heavy blur.

An unblurred copy of the figure was pasted on top of the blurred copy and then partially erased away. The opacity was also pulled down.

Going back to Selective Color, the contrast was beefed up by adding a little black to the reds and neutrals.

32   START WITH AN IDEA

Using Selective Color again, all the colors in the image were tweaked to their final hues. In the reds, five more points of cyan were pulled out and five of yellow and fifteen of black added. In the blues, −10 magenta and +20 black were the moves.

The last step was the border that extended the orange-yellow color around the top and sides. This would have been a lot simpler had I thought of it at the beginning. I could have painted it in and then blurred it with the initial Gaussian Blur.

The Canvas Size command is used to increase (or decrease) the pixel dimensions of the original file. I sampled the color from the figure, set this to the background color, and used Canvas Size to increase the shot by a quarter inch all around. The additional canvas always comes in as the background color. The Rubber Stamp was used to extend the various tones of the floor out through this new border. A feathered selection encompassing only the outer periphery of the shot was made prior to another Gaussian Blur.

I use the technique discussed here quite a bit. It's a simple but useful edge-burnishing technique. It can be done in several ways but here is the one that has the most consistent results. Open the image that will get the edge treatment. Take the Square Marquee and set the feather radius to about 30. (This number will depend on the resolution of the image.) Place the cross-hair cursor in the upper corner of the image so the top and side of the cursor just kiss the edge of the image. Click and drag down to the opposite corner and place the cursor in a similar way before releasing the mouse. Choose Inverse from the Select column and you're ready to delete, darken, lighten, fill, whatever.

The final image, complete with border.

SELECTIVE FOCUS
GETTING THE EFFECT YOU WANT

DEPTH OF FIELD is such a great tool when used effectively. But when you photograph all the elements of a computer-manipulated image, it would be silly to shoot any of them out of focus. They can always be blurred later if need be. The result, at least with me, is that I too often end up with images in which everything is sharp. I sometimes forget to take advantage of focus control because I'm so busy trying to bring everything else together.

Here's a Gaussian Blur exercise that I think you will like. It is easy to do and has a big impact on the image. You are going to create a graduated mask through which the Gaussian filter will be applied. The effect has a more photographic look than a computer-driven one. Hopefully, it will inspire you to incorporate focus control into your images. At the moment, it's all the rage in many TV commercials, too.

For my example, I have chosen a portrait with a distinct foreground and background. If the image you experiment with has no layers, you'll need to make and save a path of the foreground object.

Start by activating Quick Mask, by hitting the letter Q or the Quick Mask button near the bottom of the Toolbox. Notice that the colors in the Toolbox switched to black and white when Quick Mask was turned on. With Quick Mask, think of these colors in terms of opaque and clear. Where the mask is more opaque, the filter will have less effect. Where the mask is more clear, the filter will have a stronger effect.

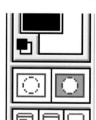

The Quick Mask button in the Toolbox. Hitting the letter Q on the keyboard achieves the same thing.

Next choose the Gradient tool and set it to Linear Blend. Black should be the foreground color. Place the cursor near the bottom of the image or wherever you want the blurring to begin. Click and drag upward and release at the top or where you think the maximum blurring should begin. To align the blend in a perfect vertical, hold the Shift key while you click and drag.

Your image will now have a red cast on it representing the mask. Hit the Q or the Quick Mask button again to generate a selection. If you had to make a path earlier for the foreground element, go to it now. Click on the path name once to activate it, and from the Make Selection dialog box, choose Subtract from Selection. If your foreground element is on its own layer, make sure the layer to be blurred is selected. Hide the selection lines with Command-H and then open Gaussian Blur.

Based on what you see after playing with the Gaussian Blur pixel radius, you will probably want to move the selection or redo the Quick Mask. Getting the mask placed properly usually takes some experimentation.

The original shot was taken with a wide-angle lens and was completely in focus.

The final image. Progressively blurring the background through a Quick Mask selection brought the attention back to the foreground figure.

In this variation, I added the color shadow technique discussed earlier. It blended nicely with the Selective Focus technique.

CHAPTER THREE

OPTIMIZING PHOTOSHOP
AN OVERVIEW OF THE BASIC TECHNIQUES

"Whether you think you can or you think you can't, you're probably right."

ANONYMOUS

WHEN YOU SEE a really terrific car you don't say, "Wow, look at that car! That is amazing! Is that car great or what?!" You say, "*Nice* car" with that quiet, understated tone of voice that says you know a nice car when you see one. With a piece of software like Photoshop you say, "*Deep* program." But if you are just taking your first spin, you may not think so. You've seen a few menu items and some tools. Big deal. If you have been struggling a bit longer, then you know what you are up against and you are probably still calling it a *big confusing* program. Hopefully, after reading this book and getting a lot of practice, people will look at your images and say, "*Nice work.*"

To describe the Photoshop program itself could take an entire book, and a large one at that. There are some excellent technical books on the subject and I've recommended them in my Selected Bibliography. This chapter, though, will be devoted to getting you up and running efficiently with the program. It also includes general descriptions of the palettes, tools, and menu items. Many of the more important tools and adjustment palettes that are mentioned only briefly in this chapter will be covered in more detail later in the book.

RAM, RAM, AND MORE RAM

How much Random Access Memory, or RAM, is enough? Well, if you're working on images destined only for the World Wide Web, then 32 to 64 megabytes, or megs, would suffice. Web images need only be RGB at 72 dpi. Images for print work such as catalogs get a little bigger but may never need multiple layers or complex manipulation. A system dedicated to this type of work would need somewhere between 64 and 128 megs. For top-end imagery with dozens of layers, time-consuming commands, and high resolution, it's hard to have too much. A minimum is your largest file in megs times three (five being better still). A file that's 4 x 5 inches at 600 dpi, with lots of layers and channels, could easily top out at 70 to 100 megs or more. After you do the math, it's a considerable bundle of chips.

Start by setting up Photoshop to work hand in hand with all that great hardware and RAM you bought. Find the Photoshop program icon in the Photoshop folder and click on it once. Press Command-I and the info window appears. At the bottom there are two spaces for the amounts of RAM devoted to Photoshop. In the Preferred Size box, increase your RAM allocation as high as you can, leaving the last ten or so megs for the system software. This will help Photoshop run at its best. Ideally, the number you type in this space will be equal to about three to five times the size of your larger files. If it isn't, Photoshop will use its own virtual memory system to use empty hard disk space as temporary RAM. The number in the Minimum Size box can be smaller, a lot smaller if you plan on having other programs open at the same time. Despite this number being smaller, Photoshop will use all the RAM given it in the Preferred Size box unless another program is opened.

Empty hard disk space or scratch disk space is crucial, even if you have a truckload of RAM. When Photoshop does run out of RAM, it writes data to scratch disk space. But Photoshop can only use RAM to the extent that it has a matching amount of scratch disk space. In other words, if you had a gigabyte of RAM but only 20 megs of empty hard disk space, Photoshop would only be able to use 20 megs of that expensive pile of RAM.

Photoshop needs to be told where to find all this empty hard disk space. You do this in the Scratch Disk section of Preferences under File in the main menu. If you have more than one drive, assign a Primary and a Secondary disk, the primary being the larger or faster of the two. If you do nothing, Photoshop will use the start-up drive as the Primary Scratch disk.

Take a big piece of that new hard drive and set aside a partition to be used only by Photoshop. A hard disk formatting program will do this

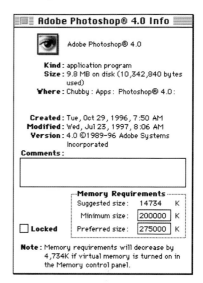

In Photoshop's Info window, assign as much RAM as you can muster to the program while leaving enough for the system software.

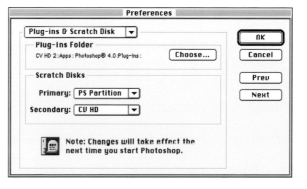

Tell Photoshop which drives to use as Primary and Secondary Scratch Disks in the Scratch Disk preferences dialog box.

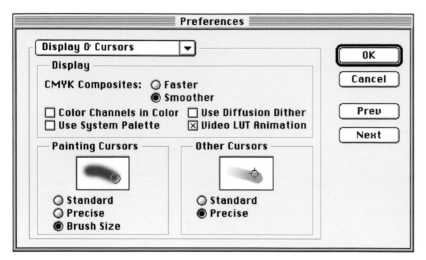

for you. The new partition will show up as a choice for Scratch Disk in the Preferences window. If you can't do this, at least optimize the drive or drives that you have assigned as scratch disks with a utility such as Norton's Speed Disk (see Chapter Seven).

Both Apple computers and Photoshop have virtual memory capability. For Photoshop to work, turn off the Mac's virtual memory in the memory control panel. While you're there, set the Disk Cache size to 96K or less. I keep mine at 64K. I have heard that you should multiply the megs of RAM you have by 32 to arrive at the Disk Cache size. This may be true for overall system use but not for Photoshop. Make sure that Modern Memory Manager is on and that the RAM disk is off.

In the General Preferences window, check the Export Clipboard box off unless you are anticipating intraprogram work. If you copy a large selection, the information is stored in RAM. When you leave Photoshop, the program will try to pass this large chunk of data on to the regular system clipboard. This may or may not work. In either case, you will have to sit there as the watch spins, if the feature is still active.

The Beep-when-Done feature was very useful back when commands took so long that you could fall into a deep sleep waiting for them to be done. Now it's annoying, so turn it off. Tool Tips, the balloon help bubbles that appear when the cursor hits things like a tool in the Toolbox, may be helpful to you early on, but shut them off when you've had enough. On the second page, check 2.5 compatibility off unless you must have it. In the Display & Cursors preferences window, I keep mine as shown above. Seeing the actual brush size on the screen is a real help.

GETTING AROUND

Photoshop gives you many ways to move around your image and the Navigator Palette is at the heart of it all. It's a fairly self-explanatory palette, if you play with it for a while, but here are some of its highlights.

Hold down the Command key and then click and drag on the proxy of your image in the Navigator Palette to define the area you want to zoom to. If you click but don't drag, you will find yourself zoomed in all the way. The color of the view box can be changed in Palette Options. Click on the black arrow in the upper right corner of the palette to access this.

Highlight the percentage in the lower left, type in a new percentage, and hit Return to go to that percentage. If you hold the Shift key while you hit Return, the percentage will stay highlighted.

Double clicking the Zoom tool in the Toolbox displays your image at 1:1. Under View in the menu, the command called Actual Pixels does the same thing. Double clicking the Hand tool performs the Fit on Screen command also found under View on the menu.

Holding down the Command key while hitting the plus (+) or minus (–) key will also zoom you in or out. If you hold these keys down for more than a second, the image zooms rapidly in or out until you let go. I find that I use these keys often, despite the more interesting ways of zooming, because they are so accessible.

The other immediately accessible way to move around your image is to hold down the Space bar and the Command or Option key for zooming in or out. Holding down the Space bar and the Command key turns the cursor into the Zoom tool no matter what tool you happen to be in. Now click and drag to define the part of your shot that you want to fill the screen with. Space bar, Option, then click zooms you out. The advantage of this and the Command plus (+) or minus (–) shortcut is that they work, even when you have dialog boxes such as Curves or Unsharp Mask open. The Navigator does not. The Hand tool also works when dialog boxes are open.

Have you ever been working with a tool, say the Rubber Stamp tool, that inexplicably turned into something else? This means: (1) you accidentally hit a key and discovered that all the tools have a corresponding keystroke (which makes rolling up to the Toolbox a thing of the past) and (2) you are like me and you would rather just start playing with programs instead of reading the manuals.

Each tool has a keystroke that allows you to select that tool to work with the Toolbox hidden. If you hit the same key more than once, the tool cycles through all its variations, if it has any. The Eraser, letter E, has four choices, for example: Paintbrush, Airbrush, Pencil, and Block. The Rubber Stamp, letter S, has seven. All the tools and their key commands are shown.

Double clicking a tool brings up the Options Palette for that tool. But why go up to the Toolbox? Hit the Return key instead. This not only brings up the Options palette, but it highlights any settings window such as Feather in the Lasso Options palette. I wish I could persuade Adobe to make a second stroke of the Return key make the Options palette go away like it did in Photoshop 2.0. Do you remember 2.0? Holding down the Control key

while clicking and holding on the image brings up a pop-up menu appropriate for that tool.

By now you should be using the keyboard shortcuts such as Command-S for save and Command-B for Color Balance. Certainly, your Command-Z keys have become glossed over from constant use. Eventually, you will get so used to these shortcuts that you will wish there was a way to assign a key command to virtually every menu item. There are two ways to do this. The first way is to use the Actions palette. The second is with a third-party program called QuicKeys, covered in more detail in Chapter Seven.

When zoomed in, nothing beats the Navigator palette for getting around the image.

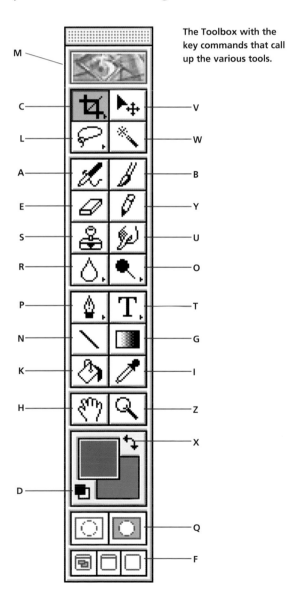

The Toolbox with the key commands that call up the various tools.

Single commands as well as multiple tasks can be put into the Actions palette. Assign an F key to your favorites.

FILE FORMATS

Just as all recorded music has a format—cassette tape, CD, reel to reel, 33 and 45 rpm records—all image files have formats. Which one do you use? Choosing a format for any image file with layers in Photoshop is easy. It can only be Photoshop format. Once the layers have been merged, however, the file can be saved in most of the seventeen choices. Those choices are Photoshop, Photoshop 2.0, BMP, Compuserve GIF, Photoshop EPS, Filmstrip, JPEG, PCX, PDF, PICT File, PICT Resource, PIXAR, PNG, RAW, Scitex CT, Targa, and TIFF. Many of these choices are dedicated to specific programs or computers. An image would only be saved as a PixelPaint file, for example, so that it could then be opened in the Macintosh program called PixelPaint. The Photoshop manual does a good job of describing these device- or application-dependent formats, so I won't do it again here.

To save that merged image, the Photoshop format is still a good choice, especially if there are saved Alpha Channels or large areas of solid color. In both instances, some compression takes place.

A TIFF file, Tagged-Image File Format, is also a good choice. You can use the LZW compression scheme with TIFF files, which causes no image degradation. A 10 meg continuous-tone image would compress to about 7 megs. Images being moved between applications or platforms often need to be TIFFs. Microsoft Word can open and place a TIFF but not a Photoshop file, for example. When saving a file as a TIFF, a window comes up in which you are given a choice between Macintosh or PC formats. The LZW compression box is also in this window.

JPEG has a powerful compression scheme but, unlike LZW, there is some loss of detail. The heavier the compression, the heavier the loss of information. A 10 meg file compresses to about 200k with Medium image quality chosen. JPEGs are good for posting on the World Wide Web or for e-mailing to clients.

EPS files, Encapsulated Postscript, are the preferred and sometimes the only way to import files into illustration and page-layout programs. To bring an image with a clipping path into Quark, it would need to be an EPS. (See Paths on page 92 for more on clipping paths.)

SELECTIONS

There will be times when adjustments to the entire image are needed. In these instances, a global change will be necessary. More often than not, though, a selection will be made first. How well that selection is made will impact the success of the modification that gets applied to it. Photoshop gives you five main selection tools: the Marquee (see page 48), Lasso (see page 50), Magic Wand, Pen tool (see page 92), and Color Range (see page 62). There are also a couple of menu options, and a host of other more subtle palettes and techniques that allow you to exert your will on targeted areas of your image. The Marquee and Lasso tools are covered in detail in the next sections of this chapter. Paths and the Pen tool have their own section, page 92 of the next chapter.

When working with selection tools, it is easy to accidentally click the mouse outside the image area. In Normal Screen mode, this mistake will click you out of Photoshop. For this reason I like to work in Full Screen mode. As a bonus, all the desktop clutter is also hidden from view.

The Magic Wand is the only main tool that I have not covered in depth elsewhere in the book. It is a rather crude tool that I use less and

The Magic Wand Options palette.

less the more experienced I become with Photoshop. If you work on very graphic images with areas composed of single colors, this tool will be very useful to you. When you click on an area, it seeks out all the pixels with similar tonal and color characteristics that are adjacent to the sample point. How it decides what is similar is determined by the tolerance level that you specify in its Options palette. If the Sample Merged button is checked, the Magic Wand will treat the image as a single layer. With it checked off, the tool will respond only to the active layer.

PALETTES

Most of Photoshop's tonal and color adjustment palettes allow you to make changes to specific parts of an image. Some, such as Replace Color, have eyedroppers for sampling the image while others, like Curves and Levels, have graphic representations of the image's tonal range allowing you to choose which part of the range to modify. Palettes with this sort of control are the ones you want to use. Simpler palettes like Brightness/Contrast and Color Balance, though seemingly easier to learn, will only wreck your images if they are overused.

Of the four dedicated color palettes—Hue/Saturation, Selective Color, Replace Color, and Color Balance—the first two are the ones that are used most frequently. (The ultimate color adjustment palette is actually Curves, which is covered on page 78.)

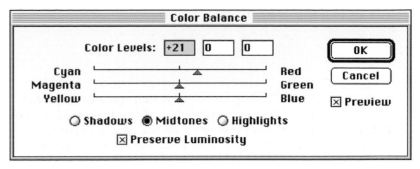

Color Balance

As mentioned above, Color Balance is crude when compared to the other palettes. When the cyan/red slider is pushed to the red side, for example, every selected pixel in the image has an equal amount of red added and cyan subtracted. Use this palette only when you want every selected pixel changed like this. True, you can specify Shadows, Midtones, or Highlights, but I find this to be a small consolation.

Replace Color

This palette doesn't affect every pixel, just the ones similar to the sample point. Like the Magic Wand, the amount of similar pixels selected is controlled with a tolerance setting, in this case a slider called Fuzziness. Multiple samplings can be added together by Shift-clicking on the image or by using the (+) Eyedropper. What I don't like about the way Replace Color works is that the boundaries between the areas it has selected and the rest of the image can be quite harsh-looking

Changes made with Color Balance are global in nature. Every selected pixel is changed equally.

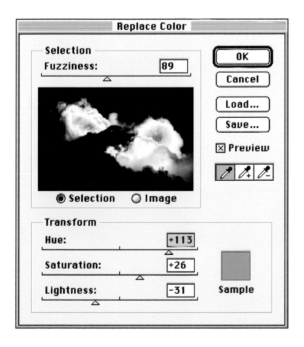

Replace Color starts with a sampling from the image (far left). All pixels in the image with a similar color characteristic can then be shifted in hue, saturated, desaturated, lightened, or darkened.

Before-and-after close-ups of an altered image (near left) show a harsh edge left behind by an exaggerated move.

once the correction is applied. In the cloud image on the previous page, I have made a large move after sampling a midtone area. Look at how raw the transition is in the adjusted side of the second image. Moves made with this palette should be subtle.

Selective Color

This next palette doesn't suffer from these problems. What Selective Color does is allow you to

The Selective Color palette with the primary color pop-down menu.

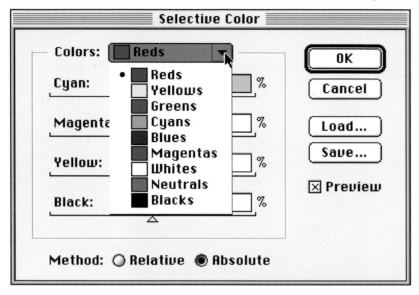

This scan has a number of areas that Selective Color can improve upon. At far right is the result of several moves in Selective Color.

change the percentages of the process colors—cyan, magenta, yellow, and black—that make up each of the primary colors. If you chose to work on the reds, for example, the amount of cyan could be reduced. Pure red has no cyan but in a scanned image of a red shirt, there will be a fair amount of cyan in the shirt. Too much cyan will make the reds in the shirt look muddy. Pulling down the cyan makes the shirt look brighter and cleaner (this is starting to sound like a laundry detergent commercial). In addition, only those pixels with a red component will be affected. The correction is very *selective*.

In the example below, I've taken a raw scan and made a number of moves in Selective Color. Cyan was pulled from the reds while a bit of magenta and black was added. Some cyan was also pulled from the yellows. The blues had magenta and cyan added to beef up the intensity. The neutrals had just a couple of points of magenta removed while some black was added. Black was added to the blacks as well.

At the bottom of the palette are two methods by which Selective Color makes its calculations, Relative and Absolute. The Absolute method adds or subtracts colors in absolute amounts. If you add 10 percent magenta to a pixel that began with 30 percent, it will now be 40 percent. This is easy to

understand and to anticipate. I have always used this method. With the Relative method, if you add 10 percent to that same pixel, it will end up with 33 percent. Ten percent of 30 percent is 3 percent. Three plus the original 30 is 33.

Hue/Saturation

This palette also has sliders for adjusting the primary colors of the color wheel. When the saturation of the reds is pulled down, though, there isn't a corresponding shift to cyan. Instead, the pixels with a red component simply become less saturated and get progressively more gray. Pushing the slider the other way increases saturation. Moves made with the Hue slider shift the color of selected pixels around the color wheel. I find that I use this slider most often in conjunction with the Colorize command.

The Colorize command can be a very useful and creative one. Checking the box turns the image or selection to shades of pure red at 100 percent saturation. From here, different hues and saturation levels can be chosen. A gray scale or full-color image can be made to have a duotone effect. The gray scale image would first be converted to one of the color modes such as RGB.

THE SAVE BUTTON

Many of the above palettes have a Save button that allows you to save the current palette settings so that they can be applied again in the future. Curves, Levels, Hue/Saturation, Selective Color, Replace Color, Variations, and Color

Range all have the button. When an alteration that you want to duplicate has been made with Curves, for example, hit the Save button before you hit the OK button. Photoshop will ask you where you want to save the template. Once saved, hit OK as usual. If many images need the

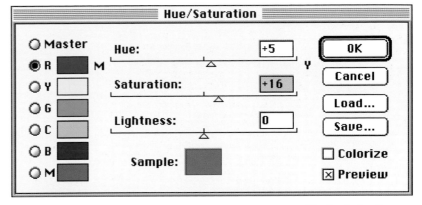

The Hue/Saturation palette.

Save early, save often. These are words to live by. But when disaster strikes and you wish that Command-Z went back two steps instead of just one, don't despair. There are a few things you can do. The first tool to reach for is the Magic Eraser. The Magic Eraser is just the Eraser with the Option key held down. If you haven't changed the size of the image or the number of layers since the last time the image was saved, you will be able to "erase" the unwanted changes back to the last saved version.

With the Eraser as your tool, click once on the image with the Option key held down. The wristwatch will appear as the file is read. You can release the Option key while you are waiting. Now hold the Option key down again and brush the saved version back into place. You can even reduce the opacity of the Eraser and partially restore the image.

The Rubber Stamp also has an option called From Saved. The advantage of using this is that you can also change the mode. You could brush the saved version back with the Rubber Stamp in Dissolve mode, for example. I've never needed to use this but maybe you will.

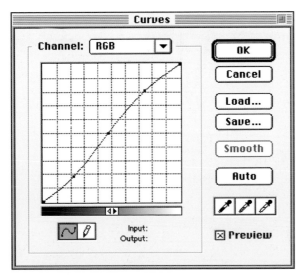

The Curves palette, like many of Photoshop's palettes, has a provision for saving new settings and loading existing ones.

same alteration, the feature will soon earn its keep.

If you only have a few more files that need an identical move and don't want to save any settings, hold down the Option key while opening a palette. The settings from the previous use will automatically be registered in the palette. Hit OK to apply these same corrections to the new image.

GETTING AROUND A SHORTAGE OF RAM

If you are working on a large file and are short on RAM, the "Not Enough Memory" message is bound to appear. Aside from purging the clipboard and closing other files, there are a few things you can do while you are waiting for those extra DIMM chips to arrive.

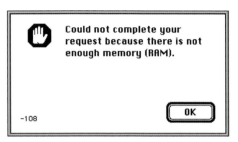

Wouldn't you like to be able to open only the portion of the image that needs work, make the changes, and then save the portion back into the whole file? Well, with certain images you can do that. Under File, go down to Acquire and over to Quick Edit. You won't see all of your files because Quick Edit can only work on TIFF and Scitex CT files. This means it won't work on images with layers.

When you select a file, a proxy of it appears on the screen. Check the grid box and then choose the number of rows and columns. Click on the segment that needs work and hit OK. When the work is done you can't save it in the usual way. You must go down under File to Export and over to Quick Edit Save.

FILTERS

Using filters can be a real thrill for the newcomer. When you are at a loss about how to alter your images, the filters oblige by twisting your pictures inside out in a hurry. My favorites are a few real workhorses. These are the Gaussian Blur, Unsharp Mask, and Noise filters.

Gaussian Blur and Unsharp Mask have associated filters with similar names like Blur More and Sharpen More. Don't waste your time with these. They're very crude compared to their big brothers.

Unsharp Mask seems to have an unlikely name. It really doesn't sharpen at all. None of the sharpening filters do. They increase the contrast along the edges that the eye interprets as increased sharpness. Since Photoshop doesn't know where your edges are, it can only look for value differences among the pixels and increase them. The other sharpening filters—Sharpen, Sharpen More, and Sharpen Edges—have no tolerance settings to help control what gets sharpened and what doesn't. Unsharp Mask has three—this is why it is the only real choice for controlled sharpening.

The first tolerance setting for Unsharp Mask is the Amount. This slider will go as high as 500 percent, but be wary of going much higher than 250 percent unless the image is very high resolution or you'll get an unpleasant contrast buildup and halos around the darker objects will result. The Amount slider determines the amount that the contrast is increased.

The second slider is the Radius control. This control determines the number of pixels away from the "edge" that are affected by the process. The higher the number, the more noticeable the sharpening will seem. For most uses, a Radius of 1 will work nicely. At higher settings, an ugly halo may begin to appear around the edges.

Threshold is like a tolerance adjustment that tells the filter how fussy it should be in determining how big a tonal difference constitutes an edge. At 0, everything will get sharpened, which

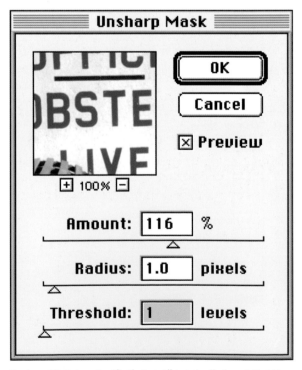

Unsharp Mask is so terrific that you'll eventually forget that the other sharpening filters exist.

Time to go RAM shopping.

will probably cause noise in areas (1) that didn't have any and (2) where you didn't want any. Going to higher numbers constrains the filter to real edges.

The Unsharp Mask filter can be slow. To save time, select a small area with the Square Marquee, zoom in to the selection, and try out the settings on this test area. After going back and forth a few times with Command-Z (to view the effect), undo the filter, deselect the Marquee, and apply the filter to the entire image by hitting Command-F. Command-F applies the most recently used filter complete with its last settings.

Although the Gaussian Blur palette only has one slider, it still beats the Blur and Blur More filters. The Gaussian Blur filter blends the value of

Left, the original image before sharpening. The details below show the original (left), after oversharpening (middle), and after moderate sharpening (right).

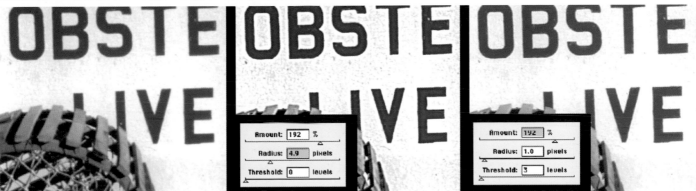

selected pixels with surrounding ones. The farther out from each pixel it looks, the bigger the
blur. This is what the Radius slider determines.
The Radius slider will accept not only whole
pixel values, but fractions as well. The fractions
are only needed at the low end of the scale, par-
ticularly below 1.

When would you need to blur something to a
radius of less than 1? Let's say you have just
retouched an area of a photograph by brushing
some color over it. That brushwork won't exactly match its surroundings because of the grain of
the photo. No problem; add some Noise with the
Noise filter. But the Noise is very sharp, sharper
than the nearby grain of the photo. Enter the
Gaussian Blur filter set to a fractional radius, .5
say. The noise just gets the edge taken off and
now matches the photo.

Blurring background elements to induce some

selective focus would be one use of a higher setting. Blurring duplicate layers to make an unusual drop shadow might be another (see page 52).

Several of the Artistic filters produce a pleasing look when applied to a lower-resolution
image. Before offering the look to your client,
make sure that the same results can be had with
a higher-resolution file. The effect may look different, take longer to get, and prove to be more
difficult to achieve than you anticipated. I was
asked to complete a job that was begun by a
designer in-house. The comp that the client
approved was done exactly this way, with a filter
on a low-resolution image. Although I got
through the job, it was painful.

As I mentioned earlier, Photoshop is a deep
program and you could fill a thousand pages
describing it. Descriptions of topics like Curves,
Levels, CMYK conversion, separations, and the

Be careful when making big gradient blends in RGB if the
image is to be converted to CMYK. Banding, heavy at times,
might be in the forecast if you do. You would think that
blurring the area would work but it doesn't. You'll either
have to work in CMYK and create the blend there or add Noise to the
area. Some filters, mostly the third-party plug-ins, don't work in CMYK.

Large
gradations
look great
until you
convert to
CMYK and
the banding
appears.
The fix is to
create the
gradation in
CMYK. If
that is not
possible,
add noise to
the blend.

I love working on images in the computer but I hate when the result looks like a computer did it. Often, when a filter, gradient, or some other technique is employed, it has a raw (computer-looking) appearance. I'll do whatever I can to blend the change into the image.

A simple example is a Motion Blur. The element is copied before it gets the blur. The copied version is then pasted on top of the blurred one. See the motion blur sample below. Would you leave it like this? Probably not. You might take a soft Eraser with the opacity pulled back some and nibble away at the edge of the original element closest to the blur. You might also go to a much larger brush, pull the opacity of the Eraser back even further, and make half or more of the element a little transparent so that the blur shows through.

You can even use this technique when applying a filter to the entire image or layer. Make a duplicate layer above the target layer or image. Apply the filter to the original. Reduce the opacity of the duplicate layer to around 50 to 70 percent. Now selectively erase this layer to reveal the fully filtered layer below. Perhaps you will softly erase over just the highlight areas, or the shadows, or around the periphery of the image.

The basic Motion Blur gets the point across (above left), but why stop there? Gently erase the back edge of the top layer to blend the two layers (above right).

Clicking around the image in an organized, search-pattern fashion is the best way to make sure that every part of the image has been checked closely for dust, flaws, or whatever.

THE MARQUEE TOOLS
SELECTION TOOLS EXTRAORDINAIRE

THE MARQUEE IS NOT one tool, but several: the Square Marquee, the Ellipse, Single Row, Single Column, and the Crop tool. The Square Marquee can often be the primary selection tool but I find that I use it more for cleaning up other selections. For example, I may have used the Magic Wand or Color Range to select a sky but the selection breaks up toward the upper corners, so I slide the Square Marquee across these areas while holding the Shift key to add to the selection.

If you are currently updating to Photoshop 4.0 from an earlier version, one of the first things that you'll notice is that most of the key commands associated with the selection tools are different. The Shift key is still used for adding to a selection but the Option key is now the one to be held down while removing parts of the selection. Moving a selection without moving the underlying pixels is easier now; just click and drag with a selection tool. Holding the Command key while doing this cuts the selected pixels and creates a Floating Selection. Command-Option clicking and dragging across the image creates a copy of the original selection.

THE SQUARE MARQUEE
In the example below, I want a selection that is feathered on one side and hard-edged on the others. A Lasso feathered to 15 pixels makes the initial selection, and then the Square Marquee with the Option and Shift keys held down makes the final selection. This is the Intersect Command. Any pixels outside the second selection are discarded and only the pixels common to both selections remain. I could also have sliced off the top and the side of the Lasso selection in separate moves of the Marquee with the Option key held down.

The above moves assume the feather radius of the Marquee is set to zero. A feathered Marquee would leave behind a soft but straight-sided selection. To change the feather radius of either tool, open the tool's Options palette and type in a new pixel radius number. In Photoshop 4.0, the maximum radius for each is 250.

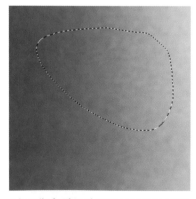

A heavily feathered Lasso made the initial selection.

With the Shift and Option keys held down, the Square Marquee is dragged across the image, encompassing part of the Lasso selection. The result is a selection at the intersection of the two.

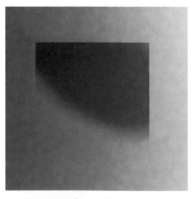

Curves was used to darken the selection and show its edge qualities.

THE SINGLE ROW AND SINGLE COLUMN MARQUEE

If you need to zoom in extremely close, in order to make sure the Square Marquee begins on a certain row or column of pixels, you may find it easier to use the Single Row/Column Marquee. With this tool, a simple click of the mouse makes a single, one-pixel-wide selection all the way to both edges of the image. This may be a longer selection than you need, but deselecting the excess is quick. Switch back to the regular Marquee and Option-select to remove the offending part of the selection. Holding the cursor up against the edge of a zoomed-in image and watching it creep across your screen is slow.

THE ELLIPTICAL MARQUEE

The Square Marquee cannot begin or end outside of the image area, but the Elliptical Marquee can. Switch to full screen mode. Make your image somewhat small on the screen. Place the cursor well to the side or top of the image and then click and drag through the image. This will give you large, graceful curving selections. To constrain the Elliptical Marquee to making perfect circles, hold down the Shift key. To make an ellipse that grows outward from the center, hold down the Option key. To make perfect circles that do this, hold down both the Shift and Option keys. These key commands render a similar result with the Square Marquee as well.

When no other selection exists on an image, holding down various keys forces the Square or Elliptical Marquees to behave a little differently. Holding down the Shift key constrains them into perfect squares or circles. Holding down the Option key makes the Marquees grow out from the initial click point. Holding down both the Shift and Option keys makes perfect squares or circles that grow out from the click point.

Under Style in the Options palette you'll find Constrained Aspect Ratio and Fixed Size. Plugging numbers into the Width and Height boxes of the Constrained Aspect Ratio window causes the Marquee always to describe a selection that reflects these proportions, no matter what the size. The Fixed Size option allows you to determine the exact proportion *and* size of a Marquee selection. Typing 72 and 72 in the Square Marquee height and width boxes would render a selection that is always 72 pixels by 72 pixels regardless of the resolution of the file. On a 72 dpi file that would be a 1-inch-square selection.

THE CROPPING TOOL

This tool can be chosen quickly by hitting the letter C. It will always crop the entire image, not just the active layer. Once the Crop Marquee is described on the image, it can be rotated by clicking and dragging outside of the selected area. This is especially handy when a scan is slightly crooked. Simply line up the Marquee with the element and hit Enter. Hitting Command "." (Command-period) gets you out of the current Cropping tool selection (and most other commands as well).

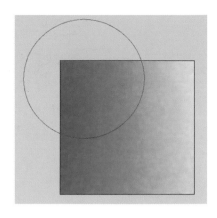

When in gray or black full-screen mode, the elliptical Marquee can be started outside the image area. The result is a large, graceful curving selection across the image. I held the Shift key down while making the selection, which constrains the Marquee to a perfect circle.

You can also crop and resize an image all in one shot by choosing Fixed Target Size in the Cropping Tool Info window and plugging in your desired dimensions. If you need to crop an image down or up to the exact size of another image, this is what you need to do. Open the source image. Choose the Cropping tool and then open Cropping Tool Options palette. Check Fixed Target Size and then hit the Front Image button. Hitting this button fills the Info window with all the dimensions and resolution numbers of the active image. Open the image to be cropped, click and drag a Marquee using the Cropping tool, and hit Enter. Don't forget to uncheck the Fixed Size button when you're done.

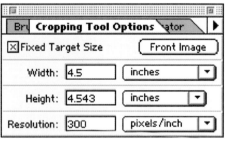

The Cropping Tool Options palette.

Don't forget that the Cropping tool can be moved and rotated. Click and drag—inside the Marquee to move it and outside to rotate it. It can be rotated up to 45 degrees but it will change size if the corners hit the edge of the image. The ability to rotate the Cropping tool is extremely helpful when trying to fix tilted scans. Simply line up one side of the Marquee with one edge in the scan that needs to come back to rectilinear and hit Enter.

When you copy a selection and then hit Command-N for New File, the size and resolution that is first offered in the New File dialog box that comes up will be the exact size to fit your copied element.

THE LASSO TOOL
SELECTION TOOL WORKHORSE

OF ALL THE MANY selection tools, the Lasso reigns supreme as the workhorse. It is the most frequently reached for tool in the box. It is probably one of the first things you played with when you got the program.

With the feather radius set to 0 and the antialias box checked off, the Lasso makes selections with razor-sharp edges. On continuous-tone images, this hard edge looks quite raw. With antialiasing on, edge pixels are partially selected, giving you a slightly feathered selection. With the feather radius set to higher numbers, you get progressively more soft-edged selections.

If you are new to Photoshop, you may not yet realize that you can have a single selection with

One selection can have many different qualities along its edge. This one began as a selection feathered to 0 and had two sections added. One was feathered to 10 pixels and the other to 25 pixels.

many different edge qualities. For example, I can make a selection with the feather radius at 0, reset the radius to 10, add to the selection, reset again to 30, and so on. You can continue to do this ad infinitum, using not just the Lasso, but all the selection tools until you have a very complex selection indeed. If this selection is one that you will need to come back to, be sure to save it as an Alpha Channel (see page 18).

I work almost exclusively in Full-Screen-with-Menu mode for a number of reasons, one of which involves the Lasso. If you attempt to click

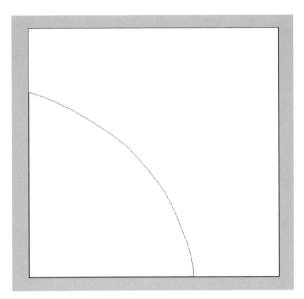

Making a feathered selection into a corner by just dragging the Lasso doesn't work very well, although it appears to at first.

and drag with a feathered Lasso to make a selection that is soft-edged in the middle of the image, but comes cleanly up against the side or corner, you will instead end up with a selection that is soft-edged on all sides as in the examples here. To avoid this hold down the Option key and set anchor points, or better still, use the Polygon Lasso. This will let you set anchor points outside the image area and give you the selection you want. If you try this in Standard Screen Mode, you will click yourself out of Photoshop and back to the Finder.

In Photoshop 4.0, to move the pixels within a selection, you must hold

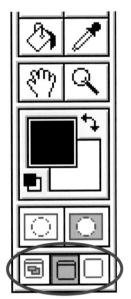

The screen mode buttons are at the bottom of the Toolbox just below the Quick Mask buttons.

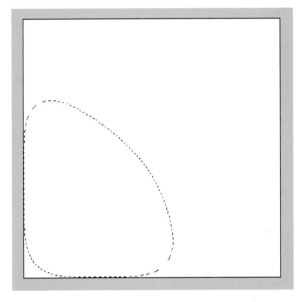

The result is a selection that is soft all the way around. If this is what you want, fine. If you wanted the selection to meet the edges cleanly, then another method is needed.

down the Command key or use the Move tool. The Scissors symbol appears next to the cursor to show that you are "cutting" the pixels out of their surroundings. Option-Shift will net you the intersection of the existing and the new selection.

The Polygon Lasso, also a 4.0 addition, makes straight-sided selections unless the Option key is held down. No need to actually complete the circuit to finish the selection, just double click the mouse or Command-click. The two open ends of the selection will close from this point on in a straight line.

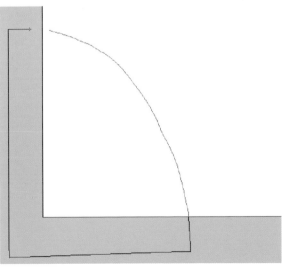

Click and drag to begin the selection but when you get near the edge, hold down the Option key and then release the mouse button. You can now make straight line segments. Keep the Option key down and set enough anchor points to carry the selection outside the image until the beginning point is reached.

DROP SHADOWS
AN ESSENTIAL ONE

EVERYONE NEEDS to do drop shadows sooner or later. Here are several that are easy to do. Some are fairly standard and some are more interesting. If you need to do drop shadows that have to look fairly standard or consistent, you might get one of the many plug-in programs that make predictable, formula-generated shadows. The steps taken to make a simple drop shadow can also be recorded in the Actions palette.

If your elements are on their own layers, basic shadows like this one are a snap.

A shadow for an element on its own layer is the simplest to make. It will take you longer to read this than it will to do it. Hold the cursor over the target layer name, hold down the Command key, and click once to make an exact selection of the layer (PS 4.0). With any of the selection tools, move the selection to where the shadow will be. From the Select column, choose the Feather command to soften the selection. The resolution of your image will determine the pixel radius that gets the effect you are looking for. Mine are generally feathered to about 25 pixels. From the Layers palette, choose New Layer. Name this new layer "Shadows" (or some such) and move it below the original target layer. Choose a foreground color for the shadow. It doesn't have to be black. Try a deep orange-brown or a dark blue. Use the Fill command to fill the selection with shadow color. Rather than playing with the opacity setting in the Fill dialog box, fill at 100 percent and then pull the opacity of the shadow layer down if it needs it (it probably will). This will give you much more control and room to change your mind later. That's it. One custom shadow.

If the element that gets the shadow is set to less than 100 percent opacity and seeing the shadow through it is a problem, add this step to the above. After feathering the selection but before filling it with color, place the cursor over the target layer name again, hold down both the Command and Option keys, and click once. This will subtract an exact selection of the element from the feathered selection.

If there is one shadow in your image, odds are good that there will be a few. I try to put each one on its own layer. If shadows from two different elements overlap, two shadow layers are needed. If you keep them on one layer, you will insult the Gods of Fate, who will make sure that your client asks you to move one of the elements, causing you to start all over with the shadows.

If the object you are shadowing is on the background, a drop shadow can still be made. You'll have to make a path with the Pen tool that describes the object. The steps are then the same as above except that the Path will be the source of the selections instead of clicking on layer names.

Here's a fun one. Make a duplicate of the layer you want to put a shadow behind. It will be created above the original. Select the original again as the active layer. With the move tool, move this layer out from under the new layer to where the shadow will be. It will become the shadow. Open Gaussian Blur and experiment with the pixel radius until you like the result. I like this method. It makes it look as though light is passing through the object and diffusely projecting it onto the background. You may want to open Curves and brighten or darken the blurred layer. If the top layer is rectangular, stroking it with a 3- or 4-pixel-wide line looks good and helps separate it from the new shadow as well.

A variation on this one is to Gaussian Blur the bottom layer without moving it. This will create a halo effect evenly around the object that can be quite pleasing. The pixel radius of the blur may need to be fairly substantial.

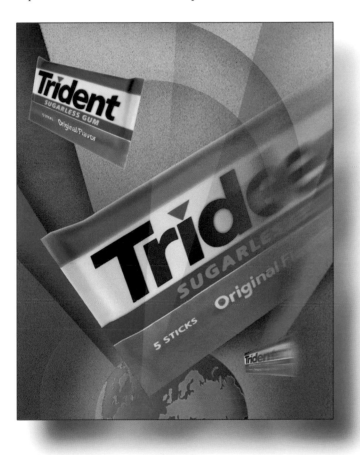

This color shadow is a refreshing change of pace. I don't get to use it nearly as much as I would like.

This is a variation on the previous color shadow. The only real difference is that the top layer isn't offset from the blurred copy below.

PART TWO

CREATIVE APPLICATIONS

Maybe there are people who were lucky enough to thoroughly learn Photoshop before they had to attempt their first real assignment. The rest of us had to dive in head first and learn the needed tasks very rapidly—on the job. The good news is that this on-the-job learning comes very quickly when you are attempting an image just a little beyond your abilities.

In this section we'll take an in-depth look at a number of my real-life commercial assignments, among them, The Lightning Catchers (the cover image), which challenged me quite a bit. Additionally, we'll continue to explore several of Photoshop's core features and tools.

CHAPTER FOUR

PUTTING IT ALL TOGETHER

A PORTFOLIO OF REAL-LIFE COMMERCIAL ASSIGNMENTS

401(k)
401(k)
401
401

Section 125

*"If at first you don't succeed,
you are running about average."*

M. H. ALDERSON

REMEMBER, you are designing a picture, not just taking one. It is no longer enough to capture what you see in your viewfinder. You now have the much more challenging job of capturing the image that's in your head. To do that you have to build the pieces, one at a time, and assemble them into a whole. You are creating images from the ground up.

To those not in the industry, the resulting pictures seem to be the work of magic. "How did they do that?" people ask. We know how they did it. They used a computer and a crafty program or two. But what happens at each step? What tricks and filters were used, and so on? Well, I'm going to tell you. In this chapter we'll take a closer look at some of Photoshop's really important, often-used core tools and features: Color Range, Layers, Curves, Levels, and Paths. We'll also pick apart four images from real-life commercial projects, including the cover image, The Lightning Catchers.

SETTING UP THE SHOT

When doing altered-reality images, such as The Lightning Catchers, a few aspects of the production need extra attention and thought. You must create one cohesive image out of many, separately photographed elements. Consistent perspective and lighting are very important. A foreground element shot with a wide-angle lens won't look right placed next to one shot with a long lens. Using the same lens on all the elements is often the key.

Sometimes, though, elements that appear small in the image, and would be tiny in the film as a result, can be shot separately with a longer lens to increase resolution. You just can't move the tripod. As an example, the two people in the cover image (The Lightning Catchers) were shot with different lenses, a wide angle for the man and a slight telephoto for the woman. The tripod stayed put. In a collage piece, this may not be as much of a concern. A huge shift in perspective may even be desired for contrast or effect.

Camera height is also important. You may find yourself "bracketing" an element from several heights in an effort to match the perspective of a previously shot element. Measuring the camera height after shooting the first key foreground elements will put an end to this.

Consistent light is another important element. In fact, the pursuit of believable, consistent light probably occupies more of my time, both behind the camera and behind the keyboard, than anything else. Ideally, all the pieces of an image are shot at once in the same light. Since this is not always the

case, the game of approximating lighting conditions gets played quite a bit. As mentioned in an earlier chapter, if the element is supposed to look like it is outside, then I shoot it outside if possible. One exception might be when the dominant light source is artificial, such as a blast of light emanating from an object close to the model. The element could perhaps then be shot in the studio. The woman in the cover shot is an example of this. Then it's just a matter matching the shadow sides to the lighting conditions in the image. I'd still rather bring that artificial light outside and have the best of both.

Something that is easy to forget when shooting elements is the effect of other objects and light sources that *will* be in the final image but are not there at shoot time. Say you are working on an image of a person in strong sunlight near the top of a mountain. You shoot the model in natural sunlight, being careful to match the direction of the sun, and then place him into your file scene of the mountaintop. If it turns out in the final that a large, sun-bathed rock were to end up appearing on the shadow side of the model, there would be some bounce-back fill light from this rock. The fill would be a cinch with the right colored card or canvas. You just have to remember to do it. This is another good argument for having a tight sketch of the final before any shooting starts.

I have a client who has me do a lot of collages, many of which have common elements. He'll say, "Take the circuit board and the globe from shot three and add them to shot eight." The long way is to select, copy, switch images, paste, and change the layer name. If you need the entire layer, do the following. Open the source and target images. From the Layers palette of the source image, click on the layer name and drag it to the target image. A copy of the layer appears in the new image complete with the original name in the Layers palette. It will be centered around the cursor when the mouse button is released. If this newly placed layer is too big or too small, the Free Transform tool can be used to change the size. If it is more than just a hair too small, it will be worth the trouble of acquiring a larger copy of the element rather than enlarging it too much. Photoshop would have to invent too many pixels that weren't there and the result would not make you happy.

Paths can be copied image to image the same way. Channels can also be duplicated and if the images are the same size, they will automatically place themselves in the exact spot the original came from.

CLASSICAL CD COVER

A SIMPLE ONE

THIS IMAGE was done for a CD cover. As this was a musician who lived some time ago, the only photographs that existed were black-and-white prints. The client wanted a lot of color added, but beyond that was open to suggestion. I decided to convert the images to Polaroid transfers to give the portrait a softer, more artistic look. I also needed some texture to hang the color onto.

The prints were photographed with Pola-pan film, which gave me a black-and-white positive slide. This slide was then put into the enlarger and projected onto 8 x 10-inch Polaroid film and the transfers made. These transfers were then scanned raw on a flatbed scanner. I say raw because I sometimes first add to them using colored pencils, pastels, and watercolors prior to scanning.

I wanted the option of having colors and elements showing through the portrait so my first step was to get the transfer onto its own layer. To do this I selected the background around transfer, selected Inverse, copied the selection, selected All, and hit Command-V for Paste. Pasting a copied selection automatically creates a new layer in Photoshop 4.0.

Let's go back to the selecting process. The Lasso couldn't be the primary selection tool, not only because of the intricacy of the edge, but because the resulting edge would have looked too uniform. I wanted an edge that mimicked the transfer: sharp and precise in some areas and soft in others. The Magic Wand was ruled out for the

 You've probably painted lines around a selection with the Stroke command. Have you ever stroked a feathered selection? Try it.

same reason as the Lasso. Color Range is the tool of choice here. If you have not yet discovered this tool, you are in for a treat (see page 62).

Often, it is easier to select the area around your target element first and then choose Inverse. Such was the case here. Color Range was used to select the unwanted background around the transfer. The only problem was that it also tried to grab all of the similar tones in the transfer. The Lasso with a small feather edge of perhaps 5 was used to deselect these areas. It was also used to grab any areas in the background that Color Range missed. Select Inverse was then used to achieve the desired selection.

With the transfer on its own layer now, Color Range was employed over and over to make "narrow" selections on the musician. These selections were then given color using the Colorize command in the Hue-Saturation palette. Highlight sections of the fleshtones were selected first. This helped me judge subsequent colors. Using the Sampled Colors mode with the Fuzziness slider kept well to the tighter-tolerance end of the scale, swaths of pixels in the area behind the musician were selected and colorized next. Because I was sampling shades of gray for each new selection, Color Range did not try to creep into the previously colored areas.

A section of page music was scanned, selected with Color Range, copied, and pasted into a layer between the background and the transfer layers. If you look at the image, the notes appear to be on top of the transfer. This was done by acquiring a selection of the notes, making the transfer layer the active layer, and then using Curves to lighten this selection. I didn't like seeing the music running across the highlighted portion of his face, however, so I undid Curves, deselected the area with a Lasso set to 5 pixels, and reapplied Curves.

This is the transfer after being cleaned up and placed.

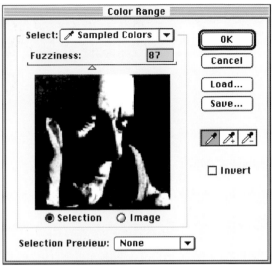

The light grays representing the fleshtones were selected with my favorite selection tool, Color Range.

Color was added to these selections with the Colorize command in the Hue/Saturation palette. To maintain the gritty quality of the transfer, no feathering was used.

Here is slice of the artist's page music.

A selection of the music layer, most of which is behind the portrait, is made from the Layers palette. After making the Portrait the active layer, Curves was employed to lighten the selection.

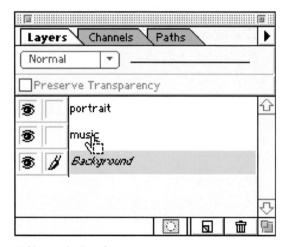

Making a selection of any layer is as easy as clicking on the layer name. As you can see here, the layer does not even have to be the active layer.

Acquiring a selection of an entire layer, such as the music layer mentioned above, is extremely easy. Place the cursor over the layer name in the Layers palette. Hold down the Command key and you will see a Square Marquee symbol appear over the pointing-hand cursor. Click once on the layer name. That's it. A selection is made of the entire layer. The layer doesn't even have to be the active layer. If there are feathered edges in the layer, the selection will have feathered edges. If you do this when there is already a selection on the image, it is lost in favor of the new one. Holding down the Shift key as well combines the selections. Command-Option subtracts the layer selection from the existing one while Command-Option-Shift nets you the intersection of the two. This trick doesn't work in pre-4.0 versions of Photoshop.

The background layer was chosen and filled with a color similar to the highlights in the face. The "burnished" edges were then added. (See page 33 for more on this technique).

The background
with its color and
burnished edges.

The final image.

COLOR RANGE
PHOTOSHOP'S MOST POWERFUL SELECTION TOOL

THIS IS MY ALL-TIME favorite selection tool. Technically, I use the Lassos and Marquees much more frequently, but their capabilities can't compare to the magic tricks I'm able to perform with Color Range. Try selecting all the bits of sky that show through a tree with the Magic Wand or the Lasso and you'll be clicking forever and a day (and it will still be a mess).

If you've never used Color Range before, this is what it does. You tell it what color or value you are looking for by either clicking on the image with Color Range's own eyedropper or picking one of the choices in the palette window, such as Highlights, Cyan, or Midtones, and so on. If Sampled Colors is the choice, you then adjust the Fuzziness slider to tell Color Range how far to the "left and right" of your target color it should look when making the selection. When you hit OK, Color Range will find every pixel within the specified "range" in your image.

If you only need Color Range to work on part

of an image, do yourself a favor and throw a Marquee around that area. Not only will Color Range work in just that area, but the preview window will show just the selection, not the entire image, giving you much better detail.

If you want to lighten all the darks and mid-tones of a shot without blowing out the high-lights, first select the highlights themselves with Color Range, feather the selection a bit with the Feather command (1 to 4 pixels generally), and then select Inverse before opening the tonal cor-rection palette you need. You can attempt to arrive at roughly the same selection using a feathered Lasso or the Magic Wand, but you'll probably end up grabbing a lot of pixels you don't want and missing many that you do. It may also cost you a lot more time in the gamble.

The subtle way in which Color Range makes its selection is not readily apparent until you view the selection by itself. The top right image on the facing page is the original and I have used Color Range to make a selection. On the bottom right, I have filled the selection with a bold color. You can see that the areas affected by the Fill command extend well beyond the selection lines. This is because many of the pixels are only partially selected. The Lasso tool, with a large feather edge, will also give you partially selected pixels, but they are arrayed in a much more "lin-ear" way. This is why changes made to areas selected with Color Range seem to blend with the surrounding areas better. Feathering the selection, as mentioned above, helps even more. I almost never use a Color Range selection that wasn't first feathered at least 1 pixel.

Using the (+) eyedropper allows you to take multiple samples on the image. Shift-clicking on the image does the same thing. There may be several shades of red, for example, that one sam-pling just won't get. If you are adding several

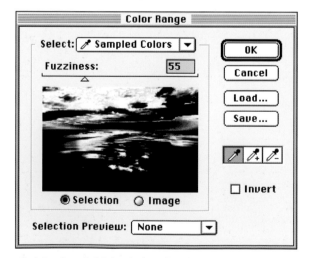

I find that Sampled Colors is the only Select mode I really use. It's the only mode with the Fuzziness slider. The other modes select with criteria that I can't control.

samples together in this fashion and go one click too far, Command-Z will undo the last sample. The (–) eyedropper (or Option clicking) will remove previously selected areas.

Color Range gives you many ways to preview the selection it will make. With Selection preview set to None and the Selection ratio button checked, you would take sample points on the actual image while watching Color Range's grayscale preview window. If this window is too small for you to see, turn on the Image radio button and then choose one of the Selection Preview modes such as Quick Mask. Now you would take your sample points off Color Range's color preview window while judging the temporary mask that appears on the actual

image. The part of your image that isn't covered by the mask represents the selection that will finally be generated once you hit OK.

There is no need to always apply Color Range to the entire image. It will work within any selection that is on the image when it is opened. Only that portion of the image is displayed in its preview window.

There is one small quirk with Color Range. It will treat your image as if it were on one single layer. If you need to select an area, part of which is hidden behind a covering layer, Color Range won't give you the selection you need. Simply turn off the offending layers before opening Color Range.

Color Range finds all the pixels in the image, based on the parameters you give it.

The four preview modes are Quick Mask, Black, White, and Grayscale.

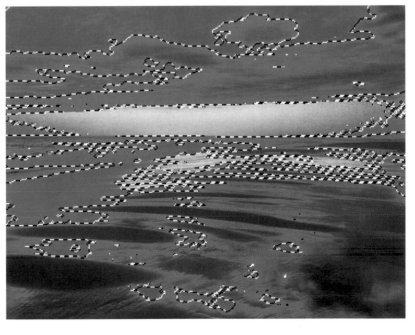

You can see that in addition to the fully selected pixels in the selection, there are many partially selected ones around the periphery.

HANDS IN SPACE
AN IMAGE WITH MULTIPLE USES

THIS SHOT was originally done for an annual report. The assignment was to show the global reach of the clients' products. I love assignments like this. They're fun to do and they can very easily be turned into good stock shots. The version here is a "stock shot" version.

The background was created with Photoshop's painting tools. The file was first filled with a midnight blue and the Airbrush tool was then used to paint the lighter blue across the middle areas. An overall Gaussian Blur smoothed away any traces of brush strokes.

When I photographed the bottom hand, I thought it was preferable to have the hand model hold an actual object as opposed to nothing. This would help the positions of the fingers look "right" in the final image. I had the right idea but the object I had him hold was too tall and didn't have an open top. I figured I would just use the Line tool to draw my own box in the computer, and although I did this, it took a lot of noodling around to get the perspective right. I should have just cobbled together a cardboard stand-in box and then used the Line tool on a separate layer to trace its shape.

The Gradient tool will do a three-color blend, but I'm not always happy with the results. This background is a large Airbrush stroke over black. Often, this can be done on a small file and then upsampled to the final size.

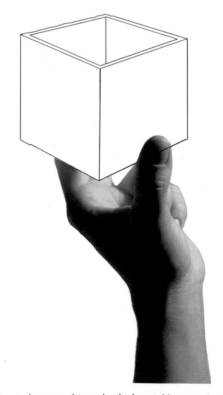

The Line tool was used to make the box, taking care that all sections were completely closed. The Magic Wand then selected one section at a time prior to pasting in the earth.

The shadow side of this hand was darkened considerably. I could have shot it with a much deeper shadow but that would have made for a difficult scan. Shooting with the computer in mind really means that your film is no longer the end product, just a raw material.

Good chromes of the earth are available from stock houses, but why pay the money and snarl up future use of the image? Use one of the royalty-free CDs or get them from NASA directly. Their web address is: *www.hq.nasa.gov/office/pao/Library/photo.html.*

The earth image I used was first rendered to a more illustrative look with a Paint Alchemy filter (see Chapter Seven). Since this earth was larger than the box I had drawn, the pieces of the earth that were used to cover the sections of the box didn't need any flattening. The easiest way to bring in these pieces would have been to select one of the facets of the box and then use the Paste Into command. Using the Paste Into command creates a Layer Mask. As you may have already discovered, this creates an element that can only be seen through this window represented by the original selection. You can move the element around behind the mask, but you can't move the window itself. I wanted an earth that could be moved about without the bother of altering any Layer Masks.

I made and saved a path for each of the facets of the box. One click on a path name selects that path and gives you a solid line on the screen. The earth sections were then pasted onto their own layer and slid around with the Move tool. When the position was right, the path was turned into a selection, the Inverse command chosen, and the Delete key hit to remove the unwanted portions. These layers were merged down to the earth layer, giving me that single element that could be moved around. A bit of Rubber Stamping was needed to blend the juncture of the various edges.

With an eye toward making things look as real as possible, I took a piece of orange mat board, scored it and folded it into a "corner," and photographed it with an orange-gelled light placed just below the lower edge of the board. This piece of film was for the glow inside the earth. I'll be the first to admit that this little exercise was a total waste of time. I should have just used the Gradient tool to add some noise. This shot was done some time ago, and I'd like to think that

Using the Paste Into command not only created a new Layer, but a Layer Mask for the layer as well.

The look so far.

I've learned a lot about when to make the effort and when to let Photoshop do the work.

The first few of the larger stars were painted in with the Paintbrush and Airbrush tools. The rest were cloned from those by first selecting them and then using one of the selection tools with the Option and Command keys held down. I could have used the Rubber Stamp tool set to Nonaligned, but the first way allows you to easily scale the size up or down, since the element is already selected. The smaller stars were simply dotted in with the Paintbrush tool.

The planets began as small selections that were filled with a blackish-blue followed by a large dose of the Noise filter. The noise was blurred down a bit before the selection was enlarged to final size. Enlarging an element rarely makes it better. In this case, the blurred noise took on a granular look that kind of worked. The selection was cut away with a feathered Elliptical Marquee and the remainder brightened to form the highlight side. The whole planet was then given a Motion Blur to give it the appearance of rotation and to hide its crude origins. One of the few rules I remembered from art class dictates that a shadow is darkest where it touches a lighter area. I kept this in mind when I gave the center of the shadow area slight brightening.

Moving an object on its own layer is easy. Moving the shadow that you burned into the layer below that object is more difficult. Rather than doing this and just darkening the skin, the shadows were made on their own layer in case the clients decided to change or remove the products (they did—and more than once). A section of the hand was selected with the Square Marquee, copied, and then pasted directly over the original selection. The shadow areas were then selected with a feathered Lasso and darkened with Curves. Sometimes filling the selection with a black or dark brown and then pulling down the opacity of the layer works very well. No matter how the shadows are made, I always put them on a separate layer.

The blurs were done with the Radial Blur filter. The items in the "drums" layer were selected one at a time, copied, and then blurred. Each blur was done in a slightly different direction. A fresh copy of the element was then pasted onto a layer over what became the "blur" layer. The trailing edge of each product was then partially erased with a soft brush and the Eraser opacity set to 75 percent.

Radial Blurs are RAM hogs. If you don't have as much RAM as you'd like, you may find it necessary to bring the element to be blurred into its own file and blur it there. If the element is large, you may even have to reduce its size, blur it, and then res it back up again. If the blur is heavy enough, you can get away with it.

As I already mentioned, shots like this are easily turned into stock shots. What else could be shown pouring into the globe? Paper money, cars, people, and so on. So many choices, so little time.

Painted planets.

The blurred drums were placed behind the clear drums on a separate layer.

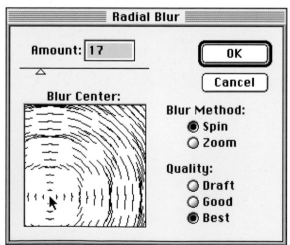

When using the Radial Blur filter, don't forget that you can relocate the center of the Spin or Zoom by clicking and dragging on the window.

LAYERS
THINKING IN THREE DIMENSIONS

SOME PEOPLE take to working with layers right away while others are initially confused by them. If you count yourself among the latter group, don't worry. Patience and persistence will get you up to speed before long.

You've probably heard this analogy, but it's a good one so I'll use it here. Think of the layers in Photoshop as sheets of clear acetate, suspended one above the other. A layer is created each time you use the Paste, Paste Into, Type tool, or New Layer command. You can add an infinite number of layers.

The Move tool allows you to slide the selected layer around the image, independent of the other layers. Clicking once in the empty boxes to the left of the layer names links those layers with the selected layer. They will now all move in tandem. They will not, however, scale or rotate together.

You can also change the order of the layers whenever you want to. Drag the layer name up or down. A heavy black line indicates where the layer will "drop in."

I find myself playing with the Opacity slider on the Layers palette quite a bit, especially with collage work. After moving the opacity around several times, it's often hard to remember where it was originally. For this reason, when I get the opacity to where I like it, say 75 percent, I will make that number part of the layer name as a reference.

To quickly change the opacity of a layer in increments of ten, touch one of the numeric keys on the far right of your extended keyboard. Hitting any of those keys sets the opacity to a value of ten times the number. Hitting the 5 key sets the opacity to 50 percent, for example.

The Preserve Transparency button, near the top of the Layers Palette, is a useful, if not quirky, item. When you check the box, Photoshop will now consider the opacity of the layer, whether it is 100 percent or not, to be inviolate. The Eraser will no longer reveal what is behind the layer but will "paint in" the background color instead. Paint tools and the Rubber Stamp tool will no longer add pigment to the more transparent areas.

When would you need to use this feature? One good example of when you should put this feature to work is if a person in dark clothes, shot against a background of white seamless paper, is brought into an image. Often the white of the seamless creeps into the clothes more than the Defringe command can handle. One solution is to use the Rubber Stamp tool with the Preserve Transparency box checked. Sample a bit from the edge and then, with a soft brush hanging halfway off the element, stamp the desired tone and texture in over the white. No pixels will be added beyond the original edge of the element, as would normally happen.

Here's another good tip for layers. There will be times when you'll need to make a selection that mimics exactly the shape of a specific layer. This is quickly and easily accomplished. Place the cursor over the layer name in the Layers palette. Hold down the Command key. A Square Marquee symbol will appear over the hand-shaped cursor. Click once on the mouse. A selection of the layer is created, and not just the outline. Even empty areas within the layer, such as the insides of letters, are selected as well. If the

Command-clicking on the layer name yields a perfect selection of that layer, complete with straight and feathered edges.

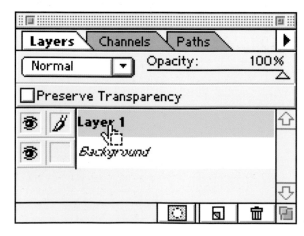

edge of an element in the layer is soft, the selection will have feathered edges. If you do this when there is a selection on the screen already, the existing one is lost in favor of the new one. Holding the Shift key in conjunction with the Command key, however, combines the selections. Command-Option-clicking subtracts the layer selection from the existing one while Command-Option-Shift nets you the intersection of the two. The layer does not even have to be the active layer. This trick doesn't work in pre-4.0 versions of Photoshop.

Have you ever needed to merge layers to accomplish some task but wished they could be kept separate for future editing? If you have, you probably accomplished this by saving a second copy of the image with the layers merged. Here's another nice layer trick that will save some disk space. Click once on the "Eye" icon to turn off all but the layers you were considering having merged. Create a new layer above these and make it the active layer. Hold the Option key down while the Merge Visible command is used. Copies of the "on," but nonactive, layers are merged and placed into the new layer in addition to remaining separate and untouched in their original layers. Enjoy throwing those extra files away.

Double clicking the layer name brings up the Layer Options palette where you can change the name or the mode, blend layers together with the sliders, and change the opacity. Since it is so easy to change the opacity on the Layers palette itself, I don't find myself doing it here too often. I also don't ever seem to change the Mode of the layer. The effects are interesting but mostly look too "computer-generated" for my taste. They are more appropriate for collage work.

If you were to reduce the opacity of a layer, the layers beneath would show through and a simple form of blending would take place. What if you only wanted the highlights of these underlying layers to show through the target layer, or just the shadows? This is what those sliders can accomplish. There are two sliders, one called This Layer, for the active layer, and one called Underlying Layer. Moving the black triangular handle for This Layer causes the deeper tones of the active layer to become transparent, revealing the layer or layers beneath. Moving the white handle causes the lighter tones to do the same. Moving the handles on the Underlying Layer bar causes the highlights or shadows of the underlying layer or layers to show through the active layer.

If you try any of these moves, you will notice right away that the resulting blend can be rather jagged or harsh looking. If you need a softer blend, hold down the Option key while moving the sliders. Only half of the triangle will move, resulting in a smooth blend. Once the triangle has been separated, the option key no longer has to be held. Experiment with different blends while choosing one of the individual color channels.

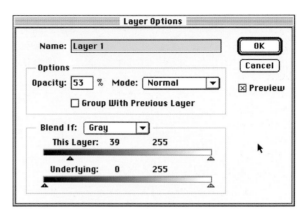

The Layer Options palette dialog box. I use this most frequently to simply change the name of the layers.

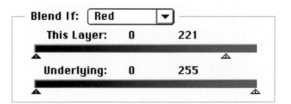

Moving the entire triangular handle makes a very jagged, posterized blend. As you can see, individual channels can be adjusted as well.

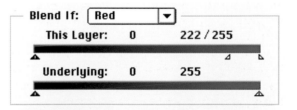

Moving half of the triangle by holding down the Option key results in a much smoother blend.

For a file with layers, the usual enemies are the plug-in filters and some of Photoshop's filters, such as Radial Blur. To get these to run on a slow machine, you may have to copy a layer or a piece of a layer, paste this into a new file, and close the original file. Now make your change, copy it, open the original file, and paste it back in. Better yet, drag the selection or layer between files instead of copying. This will keep the clipboard free.

THE LIGHTNING CATCHERS
HANGING ON TO AN IDEA

THE RAW SEED of an idea for this image started out slowly and sat around for about a year. The original idea had an older person in a field with glowing jars, but little else. What the material in the jars was or why it was glowing hadn't been worked out yet. Nor had I worked out the reason for the person to be in the field with these jars. Still, I liked the lighting possibilities and the mystery so I never let go of the image in my head. It sat there long enough for a few good thunderstorms to come, which provided more inspiration.

The elderly man holding the glowing jars is, of course, the focal point of the image. The Polaroid here shows a much frailer-looking man waiting for the signal that real film was about to be shot. He was ninety-two at the time, and is still doing well today.

The Polaroid also shows a few other interesting things; for example, the wheelbarrow is out of focus. Each of the elements had to be shot separately because of depth-of-field concerns. The field was also a lot smaller than the final image suggests. I shot the field first when the ambient light was brighter so as to retain as much of the detail and color as possible. I knew I would have to darken it quite heavily later but that would still be easier than trying to dig information out of a dark chrome.

To get the light just right on all of the elements, I elected to shoot them in the field as opposed to the studio. A heavily overcast day would have been nice. In addition to giving me more appropriate color and contrast, it would have lengthened the shooting time at dusk. The day we scheduled was bright and sunny. This was not a huge problem. We just waited for that "sweet" time at dusk when the output of the battery-powered lights in the jars balanced the ambient light at the location. It did cause me to do a bit of extra computer work, though.

In this Polaroid, Mr. Bronson waits patiently for me to decide that the light is finally right.

The empty field was shot first, before the light had fallen enough to shoot the man with the glowing jars. Had I shot it later, a lot of color and detail would not have been captured. It is much easier to darken a good file than to brighten a bad one.

For the lights in the jars, I wanted to use white Christmas lights hooked up to a generator, but the officials at the national park where the field was located did not allow generators. Instead I went with a series of flashlight bulbs connected to lantern batteries. Could I have used small strobes and a radio trigger instead? Of course. But I felt strongly about the quality of the light being just right. I knew I would get the soft, omni-directional glow from the low-tech bulbs so I went with them. The jars were lined with Roscolux Tough Spun paper to help spread the light.

Though the light was fading, I chose to shoot the wheelbarrow next. The balance of ambient light to artificial light was more important here than on the woman. She was photographed with a single LumeDyne strobe placed above the end of the lightning rod. The best part of dusk had past at this point but because she was lit predominantly by the strobe, it was less of an issue.

She could have been photographed in the studio. The jars in the field were shot last.

The clouds, fence, and trees all came from my files. The lightning was graciously supplied by a photographer buddy of mine, Phil Degginger. Shooting some of my own, to have on hand, is on my ever-growing list of things to do.

Getting the electricity in the jars was a lot trickier. The challenge of making the electricity look real nagged at me from the very beginning. I wanted it to look like it was creeping around inside the jars, popping and crackling all the while. Thoughts of using those novelty spheres, whose feathery streams of orange electricity gravitate toward your hand, were quickly written off. I was too worried it would look exactly like what it was. Scaling down the lightning bolts and putting them in the jars seemed like a good idea but only resulted in jars full of lifeless white sticks.

Though the wheelbarrow was in these frames, I ended up shooting it separately for depth-of-field concerns.

I only had three jars
rigged so the fourth
would have to be
cloned. The outside of
the wheelbarrow was
darkened considerably
to accentuate the glow.

Jean Lee, my model
here, is a historian and
librarian in my
hometown. The light
had fallen quite a bit
by the time I shot the
picture. This only
helped the look of
extreme light that I
was after. I did have to
lighten a piece of the
field, though, to
expand the area of
bright grass.

The answer finally came from "Mr. Lightning Catcher" himself, Mr. Bronson. (He still lives on the street where I grew up.) In addition to careers in photography and engineering, he is a tinkerer and inventor with many patents to his name. He has a tool he calls a hot stick. It looks like a big electric bee stinger or like a flashlight with a power cord on one end and a three-inch metal probe on the other end. It's designed to detect leaks in neon tubing. The gas lights up in the pres-ence of the current. Anyway, he suggested that I try using this thing to create the electrical effect in the jars. Touching it to anything metal causes a spark to leap from the end of the probe and run across the metal. After testing several types of metal, I went into the darkroom, pulled out a piece of film, put the metal face down on the film, and ran the probe along the edge of the metal and contact exposed the electricity. The film was cut, mounted, and scanned.

The jars were selected with the Pen tool and the grass with Color Range. The two selections were combined and this new selection was copied and pasted into a new file. Here, much of the black that came with the grass was selected with Color Range and erased with a soft Eraser.

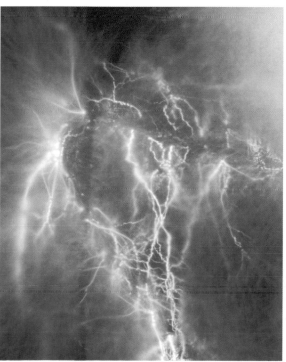
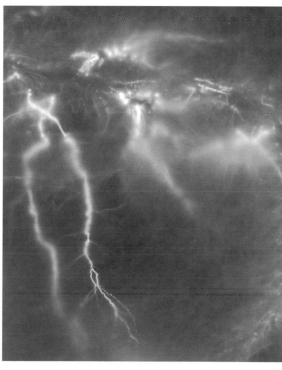

Actual electricity was contact-exposed in the darkroom.

TO THE COMPUTER

The empty field was scanned and sized to 4 x 5 inches x 600 dpi. Using Curves, the contrast and brightness were brought down considerably. Though there was much more to do, I waited until the other elements were placed into the shot to better judge the color and tonal relationships.

Next came the job that is really the only thing I don't like doing in Photoshop, making paths with the Pen tool. One or two paths is bearable, but a whole stack of them is enough to make me crazy. I try to hire this out if the job allows.

The two people and the wheelbarrow were pasted into their own layers and scaled to size. Even without the electricity in the jars, it was very

apparent that Mr. Bronson was going to need a lot of work. Shadows were too light and the glow from the jars was not strong enough. I was tempted to dig in and begin this process but a few more elements had to go in first.

I decided that the sky and the field would have more prominence and depth if the trees were removed. A careful selection of the new sky area was made. A hard edge between the sky and the grass would have looked wrong, so this division line was kept soft. Storm clouds from my files were then scanned and dropped in using the Paste Into command. These clouds had the right color but were bland and indistinct. This layer was turned off while I tried another cloud shot. These new clouds were dark on their undersides

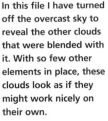

In this file I have turned off the overcast sky to reveal the other clouds that were blended with it. With so few other elements in place, these clouds look as if they might work nicely on their own.

and very bright elsewhere. They had lots of contrast and detail but were distracting and didn't look enough like proper rain clouds. On a whim, I turned both layers on and brought the opacity of the upper cloud layer down to 50 percent. This was the answer. The result was a cloud deck that had both detail and a dark, menacing color.

The rounded, upper portion of the field was cloned to the right to give it a more expansive, rolling appearance.

The last major element to go in was the electricity. Though I was happy to have figured out a way of capturing electricity on film, I was still nervous about how to bring it into the shot and make it look believable. My fears were realized when I pasted the electricity files into a slightly feathered selection of the jars. They had no depth and only appeared as two-dimensional cutouts. I tried to give it a gauzy look by reducing the opacity, but the white paper I had put in the jars showed through and made it look worse.

I realized that if Mr. Bronson's shirt could be seen through the electricity, it would look a lot more gaseous and real. In the studio, I took the red flannel shirt, placed it behind one of the jars loaded with the same bulbs, and shot a roll of film. (Times like this make me wish I had a digital camera back.) This element was then pasted behind the electricity layer. I went to this trouble because I was unsure how much of the shirt would show through. As it turned out, very little did and I could have achieved the same result (in about thirty seconds) by brushing in some red with the Paintbrush tool. Live and learn.

A separate "glow" layer was added above the electricity. In this layer I used the Airbrush tool set to about 6 percent opacity to brush a thin layer of white over the streams of electricity. The soft brush was perhaps 50 percent wider than the streams. This not only brightened it but gave it a lively glow as well. These streaks of white were not put down evenly. Occasional bends in the electricity were given extra hits from the Airbrush. This increased the popping, crackling quality.

With all of the major elements in, I was now ready to begin the long process of making them look like they belonged in the same picture. I tackled Mr. Bronson first, focusing especially on the glow coming off the jars.

Accentuating the glow from the jars required selections that only Color Range can make. To

Here, the file of the shirt has been placed on top of the jars. I was encouraged to see the luminous quality the jars were taking on even with no electricity in them.

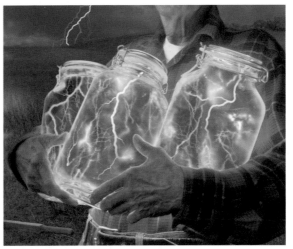

The electricity files have now been placed but are still missing the glow layer that will go in just above.

I am still amazed at how elements like this come to life when sprayed with a little white paint. The Airbrush tool set to about 8 percent does the trick.

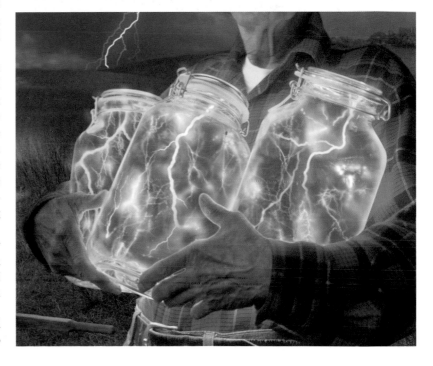

Color Range did a good job of selecting the areas closest to the glow. The parts north of the nose first needed to be bounded with a Lasso. Color Range then made selections from here, which nets a more random selection than a straight Lasso.

A busy Layers palette. If you work with lots of layers, turn off the thumbnails in the Palette Options dialog box or you will go insane waiting for them to redraw each time the Layers palette is opened.

Layers Channels Paths

Normal   Opacity: 100%

☐ Preserve Transparency

glow 68
electricity in Walt's jars
electricity in wb jars 58
electricity in field jars 44
shirt in Walt's jars
Walt
smaller jars
jar shadow
Jean
wheel barrow
fence
Lightning
trees
cloud edge
dark clouds two 45
dark clouds one
Background

constrain Color Range to specific areas such as his head, I first put a Square Marquee selection there and then used Color Range to Select just the areas of skin hit by the glow. As you can see in the Color Range palette, the upper part of the face was not selected nearly as heavily as in the lower. The resulting selection was saved as an Alpha Channel. Areas such as those under the eyebrows and around the eyes themselves were dealt with separately by first selecting them with the Lasso and then using Color Range within these selections. They were then added to the earlier ones. This final selection was then feathered to 2 pixels. Curves was used to brighten the selection and Selective Color was used to pull some cyan from the reds and yellows. This further livened up these areas. The selection was saved as an Alpha Channel since I knew I would be back here again many times before it was all over.

It was quickly apparent that the parts of the face not included in this initial selection would need to be made darker. This was done with Curves. Other parts of Mr. Bronson received similar attention. The shadows sides of the shirt and pants were deepened along with the backs of his hands. This accentuated the lighting from the jars' rims and also helped with the overall look of the ambient light. Once again, all of these selections were saved as Alpha Channels so that I could go back and tweak them all into a cohesive image later.

When I got tired of tweaking, I worked on placing some of the smaller elements. The lightning bolts were dropped in on their own layer below the existing Glow layer. The Airbrush was then used to add the same phosphorescent effect to the lightning

bolts that the electricity had gotten. A section of cloud came with the bolt that dives in and out of the clouds. The color of this cloud section was adjusted to match the Color Balance palette.

A few trees from my files were dropped in. The fact that they were made to look small helped to make the field seem still larger. The fence was also from my files and I used the Perspective command on it to make it match the pitch of the field. The tops of the two posts nearest the woman were brightened to the point of being almost white. The side of the one was lightened as well. This original fence was backlit by a sunset so there was no detail to bring out. I used the Burn/Dodge tool to give the lightened side of the post a slightly uneven look. The net result is a post that is more "painting" than photo. I only got away with it because it was so far in the background. A post next to Mr. Bronson would have to have been lit and shot.

The jars along the path near the woman gave me some trouble. Because they were shot in almost full darkness, the shadow sides of the grass were dead black. When placed into the shot, these black shadows looked out of place next to the grass of the field that was shot much earlier. I used Color Range to select the shadows, feathered the selection, and then erased them with a large, soft brush. Some further erasing took place after the jars were placed in the final image.

I ended up with more than twenty-five layers in this image. That made for a very busy-looking Layers palette. You may have already discovered that it takes quite a while for all the small icons of the layers to redraw. To simplify things, go into the Layers Palette Options by clicking on the black triangle in the upper right corner of the Layers palette. Choose None for Thumbnail size. This will quickly tame a large, unruly Layers palette. To see an Easter Egg, hold down the Option key while choosing Palette Options. An Easter Egg is a whimsical little surprise put into the software by the programmers. To see another, launch Photoshop and then hold down the Command key while choosing About Photoshop from the top of the Apple Menu Items column. Command-click on the nose.

I spent an enormous amount of time on this shot, but it was never boring. Seeing the image emerge and come to life on the screen made all the effort worth it. There were no clients to step in and muck it up either, since this shot was done for the portfolio.

The final image.

CURVES AND LEVELS
PHOTOSHOP'S MOST POWERFUL TOOLS

Why are Curves and Levels so much better than Brightness/Contrast? So much better that people who have been working with Photoshop for more that a year rarely ever open the Brightness/Contrast palette anymore? The answer comes in two parts.

The first half of the answer resides in the way Brightness/Contrast works. It's extremely crude. Changes made with it are global or all-inclusive in nature. When you brighten an image by pushing the slider up to 20, every single pixel is brightened the same amount. The same is true when darkening.

It's a shame that the names of the two palettes are such that beginners (at least the ones who don't like manuals) always reach for Brightness/Contrast while wondering what Curves and Levels are for. As you will see, the second half of the answer lies in the remarkable degree of control afforded by Curves and Levels as compared to Brightness/Contrast. If I haven't made the point yet, let me be blunt. When making tonal corrections to images, don't use Brightness/Contrast.

To really understand how these two palettes manipulate the data in an image, you need to understand the data itself. Let's start with the individual pixel.

Each pixel is composed of bits. The more bits, the greater its bit depth. Each bit in a pixel can be expressed as a 1 or a 0. A pixel with only 1 bit can be displayed as one of two colors, usually black or white. A 1-bit pixel can be expressed as 2 to the power of 1 or 2 times 1 is 2 shades of gray. A bit depth of 2 graduates to having 4 shades of gray; 2 to the power of 2 is 4 shades, and 8 bits or 2 to the power of 8 is 256. These shades of gray are also called levels of gray. A 24-bit image has 16.7 million colors because it has three channels of 8 bits each and 256 to the power of 3 is 16.7 million.

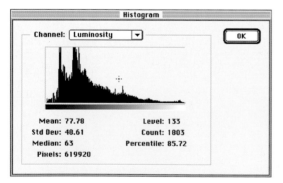

Most of the areas in this image are somewhat dark and the Histogram reflects that. Placing the cursor on or above the bars or levels provides a pixel count for that level.

The three color channels mix to make new color combinations, but not new levels of brightness. This remains at 256.

A Histogram is a graphic representation of these brightness levels at each color and the number of pixels at each level. The value of each level in an RGB image is described by a number starting with 0, which is full black, to 255, which is pure white. That again is a total of 256 possible values.

Two images and their Histograms are shown here. You can see that the bulk of the pixels in the picture on page 78 are in the darker midtones and blacks. If the cursor is placed on or just above the bars, the number of pixels at each value can be read. In this Histogram there are 1803 pixels at Brightness Level 133. Histograms for the individual channels can also be viewed.

The second file, shown below, was filled with a single color. As you might expect, the Histogram is a rather simple one. All the information resides at Brightness Level 120, shown by the single bar in its Histogram.

Levels and Curves make tonal and color corrections in a controlled way. The adjustments can be applied to specific value ranges or levels while leaving other areas alone. In short, they do largely the same thing. The Levels palette is easier for the novice to understand because of the relationship of the sliders to the Histogram. For that same reason, I find it much easier to use for certain things, such as setting the black and white points.

The three little triangles just under the Histogram are the Input Sliders. Moves made with them are quantified in the boxes above. The 0 in

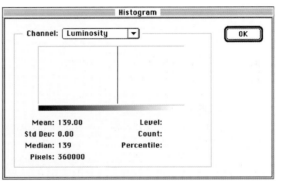

A file filled with only one color can have only one level of brightness (left). That one level is shown is this sparse Histogram (above).

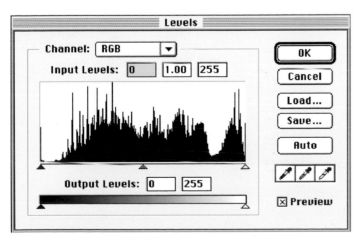

The Levels palette is easier to understand for some because of the Histogram at its center.

the box on the left represents Level 0 or pure black. Moves made with the black point Slider are reflected here. In the box on the right you see 255 for pure white. The center slider is the Gamma Slider.

The Levels palette shown here is for the image below on the right. You can see that there are not many pixels in the first few levels. The nearest grouping of pixels of any consequence begins a little to the left of the default position of the Black Point Slider. What I want to do is to move the slider to the beginning of these pixels. When I do, I see that this is level 12. All the pixels at level 12 will now become level 0, or Black, and all the levels above 12 will be reshuffled or remapped. The pixels that were below 12 are now at level 0 as well so that a little bit of detail is lost. This is called Setting the Black Point.

Setting the White Point is the same, just on the other end of the Histogram. If the slider is moved from 255 to 247, all the pixels at 247 become 255, or pure white, and the levels to the left get remapped. Pixels that were above the old 247 are all 255 and that detail is also lost.

As a result of these moves, the Tonal Range is compressed and we see an increase in contrast. If Levels is reopened, you would see gaps in the Histogram representing the lost information.

Above, the original image of Camden, Maine. At right, the white and black point sliders have been set as well as the Gamma slider. To the right of the original is the scan after the Levels adjustment.

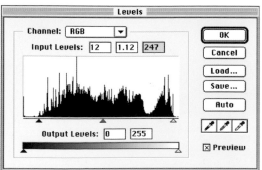

The Gamma slider adjusts the midtones without appreciably touching the highlights or the shadows. This should be done when both the black and the white points have been set. Since the levels on either side of the Gamma slider will get remapped, overly large moves with this slider will negatively impact the image. The proof is in the Histogram shown here (top right). In addition, corrections to the midtone areas can be made in a much more controlled way with Curves, as you will see.

Using the Output sliders at the bottom of the palette works very differently from the others above. If the Highlight slider is moved in from 255 to 245, every level at or above 245 becomes 245. You now effectively have fewer levels than before. Not only that, the highlights that were pure white are now a dull-looking light gray. Having a few small areas of an image blow out to paper white is fine. Until a printer I respect set me straight, I used to go around the image filling these in, thinking there had to be ink everywhere.

Working with the black slider is the same, just in reverse. The range of levels is compacted to a smaller quantity. This can be a useful tool for keeping the shadows from becoming blocked up with too much ink or for controlling dot gain, especially with Ink-Jet output.

I find Curves to be the more complete and intuitive of the two palettes to use and I therefore reach for it much more frequently. It's hard, at first, to figure out what the palette does or how it does it.

The palette seems to have a lot less going on than the Levels palette. Let's start with the grid. The horizontal axis of the grid represents the 256 levels in the image, the Input Levels. Picture a Histogram right below the grid. On the left is 0, pure black, and on the right is 255, pure white. The vertical axis represents the output brightness of those 256 levels. The diagonal line is a graphic representation of the levels getting brighter as you move to the right. If you move the cursor over the grid, you will see the input and output levels displayed.

Clicking on the diagonal line sets anchor points. If one point is set in the middle of the line and dragged upward, you will see the image getting brighter. Since the ends of the diagonal line were already anchored down in the corners, the greatest change took place in the center, or midtone, area. These levels were remapped to new and higher output levels.

If you wanted to change the highlight and shadow areas while leaving the midtones alone, you would set one anchor point on the center of the line, one a quarter of the way up the diagonal, and one three-quarters up. Pushing the three-quarter point up and the one-quarter point down would brighten the highlights and darken the shadows

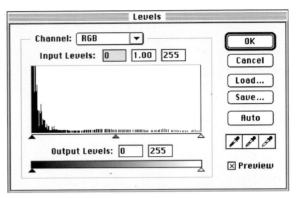

Overuse of the sliders results in the tonal range being stretched or compressed beyond tolerable limits. Here, the Gamma slider was moved too far right. The shadow side of the range is highly compressed and the highlight side stretched very thin. Breaks in the levels are easily visible.

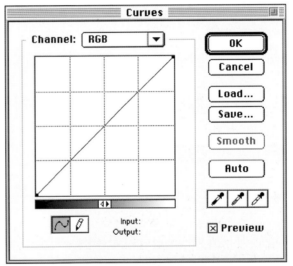

The Curves palette.

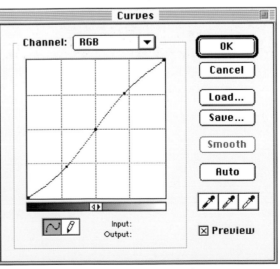

The standard S-curve increases contrast by lightening the highlights and darkening the shadows. It's a good place to start for most images, when first brought into the computer.

while the anchor point in the middle held the mid-tones steady. Again, because the two ends of the line are anchored, these moves would have little effect on the pure blacks and whites. Up to fourteen of these anchor points (including the end points) can be used so that fairly small sections can be adjusted while the rest of the line is held in place. To help you see finer adjustments, Option-click anywhere on the window to get a tighter grid.

If you wanted to make a correction to a specific part of an image, how would you know which small section of the line to adjust? With the Curves palette open, place the cursor over the image and hold down the mouse button. A circle will appear on the diagonal line that represents that part of the image. Set your anchor points around this area and then set another one where the circle was. Drag this point to adjust the image.

You can begin to see that with so many anchor points, the parts of the tonal range can be adjusted more specifically than with the three sliders in the Levels palette. Both the Curves and Levels palettes have Auto features. Clicking the Auto button automatically sets the white and black points for you. This feature offers a fast fix that works well on some images and not on other images. At the very least, it may give you a quick preview of what parts of the image need attention.

Clicking on the arrows in the center of the gray scale bar reverses the orientation of the highlights and shadows. With the shadows on the left (the default position for RGB files), the diagonal line gets pushed up to brighten and down to darken. This seems like a logical arrangement to me. The default position for CMYK files is the reverse, with highlights on the left. I'm sure there is a good reason for this but working backward seems very counterintuitive. I switch it. Be wary, though, of making large moves with Curves (or any correction tool for that matter) on CMYK images. It is possible to

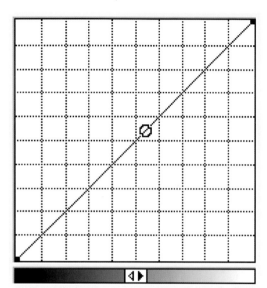

Clicking on the image with Curves open yields a circle on the grid. This circle represents where along the tonal range the pixels under the cursor are. More importantly, it tells you what part of the diagonal line to adjust.

push values past the tolerances you had described in your Color Preferences settings.

Changes made with Curves (and Levels) aren't limited to tonal adjustments. Color corrections can be made as well. In fact, this is the place to come for really good control over color adjustments. The reasons are the same as discussed above. Changes can be made to specific parts of a color channel. Highlights in the red channel, for example, could be altered while the rest of the range is kept constant. Corrections made with a tool such as Color Balance are crude by comparison. Curves can select a narrow piece of the tonal range. They're not able to select a narrow piece of the tonal range. Curves in particular can do exactly that.

Learning how to make these adjustments in the individual channels takes some practice. Moving the diagonal line doesn't cause the kind of change you might expect if you had used only Curves with all channels on previously. Moving the line with all channels on makes the image lighter or darker. Moving the line with only one color channel selected causes color shifts.

The best way to start is to have a color wheel in front of you. Open an RGB image, open Curves, and select one of the channels, say the blue channel. Drag the line down from the center. The image doesn't get darker, it gets more yellow. What color is opposite blue on the color wheel? Yellow. Now drag the line upward. The image takes on a blue cast. Moving the line up increases the percentage of blue, generating a blue cast, and moving it down removes blue, increasing the percentage of yellow and resulting in a yellow cast.

Pairs of channels can also be adjusted together (see page 85). To do this, open the Channels palette and turn off the unwanted channel by clicking in the Eye icon. Next, click on the channel name of one of the remaining channels. Shift-click the second channel. Now open Curves to make the correction.

Don't expect to become proficient with these two powerful tools overnight. Growing comfortable with them will take time and practice. Besides the obvious reasons for making the effort, consider this. Many scanners include a Curves palette in their software. If after viewing the preview image, a correcting Curve is applied before the scan takes place, less adjustment work will have to be done to the image in Photoshop. Less adjustment in Photoshop means a more intact histogram and smoother color.

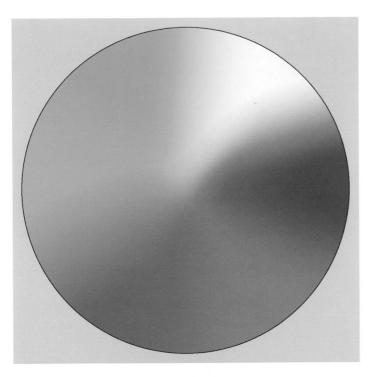

When first learning to adjust color with Curves or Levels, it is very helpful to have a color wheel available. Increasing the percentage of one color will decrease the proportion of the color on the opposite side of the wheel.

The original image has a lot of neutrals that will show the effects of adjusting individual channels in Curves.

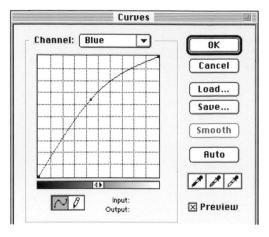

Pushing the diagonal line upward increases the percentage of blue ink and results in a blue cast.

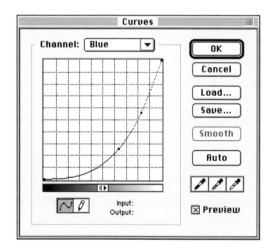

Pulling the line down in the blue channel decreases the percentage of blue, which increases the proportion of yellow, resulting in a yellow cast.

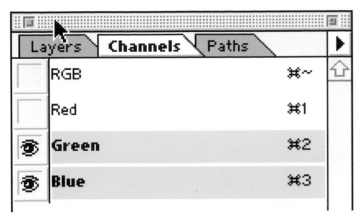

To work two channels together, open the Channels palette, click on one of the desired channels, and then Shift-click on the other.

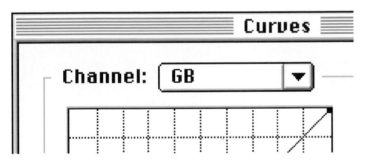

Paired channels are identified by single letters in the Curves or Levels palette. The two channels can be worked individually by clicking on the pop-down menu and choosing one or the other.

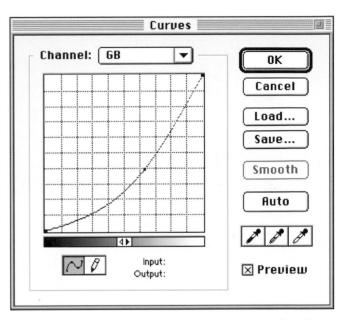

Making changes with paired channels is much the same as with single channels. If the diagonal line is pulled down, as in this case, the color opposite the pair in the color wheel is brought up proportionally, resulting in a color cast of that color.

Here we see the red color cast that resulted from pulling down the percentage of blue and green simultaneously.

 Scanners that come with powerful software such as the Agfa DuoScan allow you to apply tonal and color corrections in the scanning process. This results in an image that will need less adjustment in Photoshop. The benefit to you is a final image with a minimal loss of information and a cleaner histogram.

LISTERINE COLLAGE
PHOTO OR ILLUSTRATION?

THIS SHOT was one of a series done for an annual report. The clients wanted an illustrative look blended with a little photography to give it an "edge." I found the whole process very interesting and satisfying. It called into play many different aspects of Photoshop including unusual selections, drop shadows, color work, and retouching techniques. On another note, the shot was done some time ago in Photoshop 3.0. While I am still happy with the end product, there are things that I would do differently now. See if you can guess what they are.

To stay with the arty look, I had an illustrator airbrush a few shapes and gradients for me. I wanted the random grain of the airbrush instead of the mechanical sameness of the Noise filter. This, of course, means more work but I have

strong feelings about the way the image should look. Allowing the computer to do everything, although easier, would show in the quality of the end product. Standing out among the competition takes constant energy and growth.

The file was started with only one of the gradients. The other shapes were added after the main elements were in place. These elements were worked on in their own files and brought in only when they were largely done.

Next came the "rendering down" of the bottles. It may seem like tedious work, but I actually enjoyed retouching the Listerine bottle so that it looked like an illustration. It was a challenge to see how far I could take it, treading that fine line between photograph and painting. The initial goal was to get rid of the irregular reflections,

These cones were made by an illustrator with an airbrush. I could have easily made them in the computer but they would have looked it. I suppose to some this is not an important distinction, especially for a background element. It is to me. Images like this one are the sum of a series of details. If the details are taken care of, the shot will be a winner.

The gradation at far right was used on several images in the series. Variations were arrived at with the Colorize command in the Hue/Saturation palette.

highlights, shadows, and any other imperfections. This was achieved with one of two methods.

The first method involves heavy use of the Rubber Stamp tool. Rather than attempt a look that is perfect (hard to do on large, smooth areas), I quickly cover over the offending parts with the desired color and tone, select the area with a Lasso feathered to three, and then give the selection a Gaussian Blur to smooth it out. The amount of blur varies, but I try to use the lowest pixel radius possible that will still get the job done. Overblurring will pull too much color from outside the selection. The blur smoothes out all the grain, however, so the Noise filter is used to put some back in. Occasionally, colored noise works, but nine times out of ten it's Monochromatic Noise that does the trick. This new grain may look just a little too sharp compared to the

area outside the selection. A second Gaussian Blur of .3 to .5 pixels solves this problem.

The two larger clear portions of the bottle and the label were handled this way. The label needed extra selection work, though. I first selected the large black letters with the Magic Wand and saved the selection. Using the Pen tool, a path for the entire label and of the shape in the label under the black letters was made. I could then work on the individual areas and also isolate the white by converting the path of the entire label and subtracting the other two.

The second method is a lot faster but, unfortunately, can't be used all the time. It employs the Gradient tool to completely paint over areas using colors taken from the element itself. The side of the Listerine bottle had ugly highlights, a seam, imperfections, and so on. I selected the

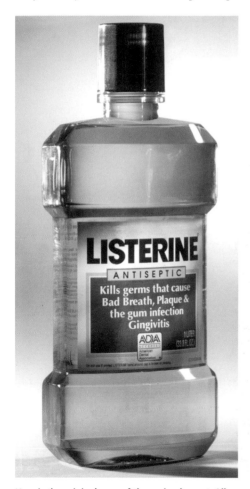

Here is the original scan of the main element. All the imperfections, such as the rear label showing through, needed to be retouched out. The process was challenging and time-consuming, but satisfying.

The individual qualities of light and shadow in areas such as the large clear section at the top of the bottle were maintained during the "rendering down" process by applying a Gausian Blur. Smaller, troublesome parts, such as the sides, needed a different solution.

The solution was to select the area, sample the colors at the ends of the selection, and apply a Linear blend with the Gradient tool. A little Monochromatic Noise, followed by a slight Gaussian Blur, finished the job.

area with a lightly feathered Lasso, sampled the color at the top and bottom of the selection, made these the foreground and background colors, and put down a Linear Blend of these two colors. The Noise and Gaussian Blur filters were then used as they were before.

Once all areas had been cleaned up, Selective Color, Hue/Saturation, and Curves were all used to purify and strengthen the colors in all areas of the image. This strengthening did not take place all at once but rather in stages.

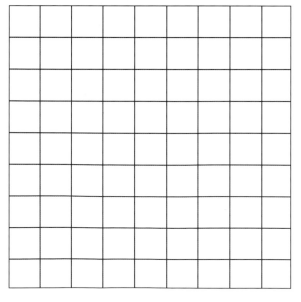

To make an easy grid, start with a single tile such as this. With the tile selected, use the Define Pattern command from the Edit column in the main menu. Use the Fill from Pattern command in the Fill dialog box to cover your selection or file with tiles (right). Now just select the grid with the Magic Wand or Color Range prior to copying and pasting the grid into an image.

When all three bottles were rendered down like this, Selective Color was used to clean up and strengthen the colors. For the main bottle, this meant pulling cyan from the yellows and reds and then adding yellow and magenta to the yellows and reds. After being saved, the bottles were brought into the collage image. Portions of two of them were deleted after first being selected with a Lasso set to a feather edge of 65 pixels.

No one wants to do the same work twice. With that in mind, I saved every element to CD that seemed like it might come in handy someday. The grid behind the map is one such element (see the final image on page 90). I only needed to shift the color.

To quickly make your own grid, start with a small file, say 4 x 5 inches by 100 dpi. Use the Square Marquee with the Shift key held down to constrain the selection to a perfect square. Make a selection that equals the size of one segment of the grid. Set the foreground color to your desired grid color. Open the Stroke dialog box and set the width to one or two and the location to Inside. Hit OK. Under Edit in the menu bar, go down to Define Pattern and release. Select the entire file. Open the Fill dialog box, choose From Pattern, and hit OK. There is your grid. The line width will be twice the number used in the Stroke dialog box.

The map came from another CD; this one from Mountain High, Inc. It's a disk full of outlines of all the countries and continents of the

GOOD ADVICE The Transform functions include all the commands you may remember from Photoshop 3.0 as well as the new darling, Free Transform. With Free Transform, you can perform any or all of the old effects of Scale, Rotate, Skew, Distort, and Perspective in one command. Since some pixel information was lost with each of these separately used commands, the ability to do them all at once is an improvement. The transformed element will retain more of its clarity and original information. Command-T activates this tool, but I use this tool so often I've assigned an F key to it with the Actions palette. The Quick Reference card that comes with Photoshop has all the key strokes for the individual commands.

Do you need a great way to measure the exact amount of rotation an element will need? Open the Info palette and then put a selection on the image with the Crop Tool. Rotate the Crop selection by clicking and dragging outside the selection. The Info palette will show the number of degrees rotated. Line up an edge of the selection with an edge of the element and use the number in the Info palette to calculate how much to rotate the element. The Arbitrary Rotate command lets you type in the exact number or the Info palette can be watched while using the Free Rotate command. Hitting Command-. (period) will remove the Crop selection from the screen.

A second way to do the same thing involves the Line tool. Open its options palette and set the line width to zero. Open the Info palette. Click and drag along an edge of the element to see how far from horizontal or vertical it is. You won't even have to Command-Z the Line tool since it won't leave a mark on the image.

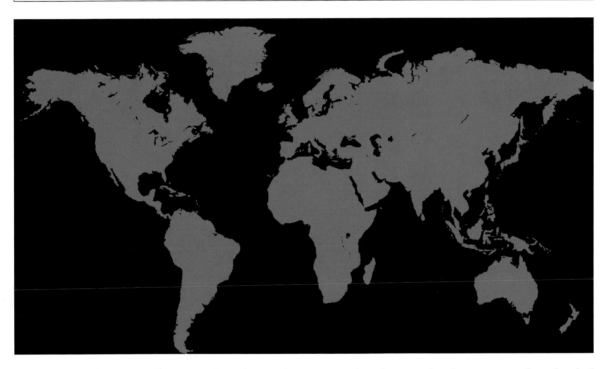

Mountain High, Inc., sells CDs full of map outlines. Some have country borders and some don't. The outlines are easily turned into plain maps. This one was placed on top of a grid, placed into the final image, and given a shadow, a Linear Blend, and some Noise.

world. A world map outline was placed onto the grid file and the continents were filled with a bright orange. The layers were merged and this file was next pasted into the collage image.

The strong perspective would have been made with the Free Transform function but it didn't exist in Photoshop 3.0. The Perspective and Free Rotate effects were applied separately. Photoshop 4.0 still has all the individual effects such as Scale, Rotate, Distort, and so on, but I don't use them much. Free Transform does it all.

The continents were left solid orange up to this point to make selecting them easier. With the other layers turned off, Color Range was used to make this selection. The selection was saved, moved up and to the right, and then feathered to

15 pixels. The saved selection was then loaded and subtracted from the feathered one. Curves made short work of deepening the grid to produce the drop shadow. I made the shadow at this stage, instead of when the map and grid were in their own file, because it produces a more three-dimensional look.

The saved selection was reopened and the continents were given a Radial Blend of light and dark orange and 20 points of Noise. The last thing left to do was to nibble away at the edges with a large, soft Eraser set to 50 percent opacity.

Several of the cones that the illustrator made were selected with the Lasso and then brought in. After being rotated and placed, the Colorize command in the Hue/Saturation window was used to change the colors. I was after color complements: red and green, yellow and purple, blue and orange. The two cones to the far right and left each had one of their edges erased away with a large, soft brush.

The circular shapes are just colorized selections in the original background gradient. After the initial selection was made with the Elliptical Marquee, most of it was removed with the Lasso set to 70 pixels. The light, wedge-shaped area on the large bottle was done with Curves after first taking the selection from the cone beneath.

As a final touch, a shadow was burned into the background behind the sides and top of the main bottle.

There are a few things I would have done differently: (1) I would have made Layer Masks to hide portions of the product and map instead of actually erasing them; (2) I would have used Adjustment Layers to make the light wedge on of the main bottle and the shadow behind it; and (3) I would have completely finished the map/grid element in its own file and saved it.

The final image has an amount of color saturation that I don't often get to use on product shots.

When asked to retouch a small area of an element, for example, removing some text from a label, most people reach for the Rubber Stamp tool. You've probably noticed that problems, such as repeating or blotchy patterns, frequently occur. Here is another retouching method that results in a smooth, seamless appearance.

The first thing to do with the Rubber Stamp tool is to sample from several random points, not just one. Fill the area in, matching the tone, texture, and color as best you can. Don't worry that it's not perfect. Next, with the Lasso set to 2 or 3 pixels, make a selection tightly around the area. Now give the selection a Gaussian Blur. Don't blur it so heavily that you pull color in from outside the selection. You just want enough to smooth out the bumps and blotches. At this point, the only thing it will appear to be missing is grain. Open the Add Noise filter dialog box, and set the amount so that the size of the new grain matches the area outside the selection. The Monochromatic box may also need to be checked on. This new grain will most likely look too sharp so the next step will be to give the selection another, very slight, Gaussian Blur—.4 to .5 will usually do the trick.

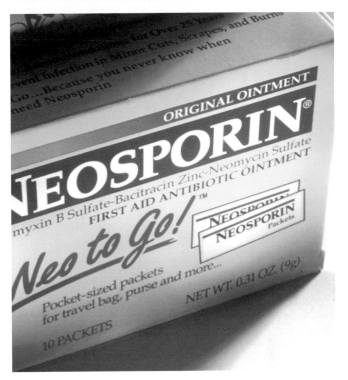

Retouching a section of type that runs in and out of shadow can be tricky. The process in this example begins with the Rubber Stamp tool.

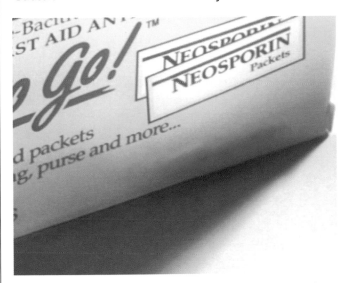

The goal at this stage is to cover the type with tone that closely matches the desired tone. Don't worry about getting it exactly perfect. The next step will take care of this.

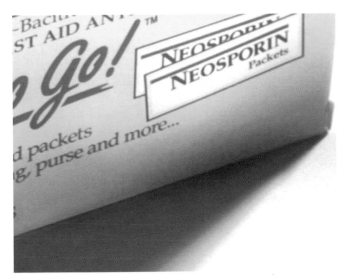

Here the retouching is finished. Had the type not been partially in shadow, it might have been possible to use the same soft Lasso, select a similar area of the package, and copy-drag this selection onto the type to cover it. The finishing steps would be as before.

PATHS
BUILDING A SELECTION BY HAND

BACK IN THE DAYS of Photoshop 2.0, paths were everything. There were no layers. Pasting Into and Pasting Behind were popular commands. Saving a path for almost everything was the way to go. I use paths much less frequently these days. There is one place, though, that I still use the Pen tool as much as ever: making a path for a newly scanned element that needs to be copied into the target or final image. Occasionally, I'm able to get away with using the Magic Wand if the background is clean, but usually it's the Pen tool's job.

The Photoshop manual shows a similar example to the one I've shown on the facing page being done with one curving segment. That method uses one less anchor point, but several more keystrokes.

A path can be more than one closed circuit. You can make many closed circuits at once and save them all as one path. Just be sure to Command-click on the image someplace (not right on the path itself) to deselect the anchor points. To remove single anchor points, hold the Control key down while clicking on the offending point. You can also choose the Minus Pen tool from the Toolbox. Control clicking between existing points will add a new one.

If you select a saved path by clicking once on its name, add a new series of points, and then deselect those points by again Command-clicking on the image, the new path automatically becomes part of the original one. No Save instruction is needed. Command-clicking on a saved path makes the anchor points reappear. They can now be moved with the white arrow pen tool or by holding down the Command key.

Using the Make Selection dialog box from the Paths palette, individual paths can be loaded and feathered. Additionally, several paths can be loaded together, one can be subtracted from a selection, or the intersection of a path and a selection can be arrived at.

If you have a selection on the screen and would like to save it as a path, you can do it from the Paths palette. Click on the black triangle at the upper right of the palette and scroll down to the Make Work Path command. A dialog box will ask for a pixel tolerance number. The more intricate the selection, the smaller the number needs to be. The smallest number it will accept is .5 and the biggest is 10 (Photoshop 4.0). If you plug in 3, an anchor point will be created every 3 pixels along the selection. Any detail in the selection that is smaller will tend to get rounded over. I leave it set at 1 for most uses.

You have an irregularly shaped object on a white background and you want to import it into another program such as Quark and not have its background show. This requires a Clipping Path. True, you could tell Quark to make a solid background color, such as white transparent, but you might get a ragged edge and bits of white hanging on to the object. It's not a pleasing look. Making a Clipping Path is the right answer and is easy.

Start by making a careful path around the object. Save the path by choosing Save Path from the Path palette options menu. Now choose Clipping Path from the palette options menu. In the window that comes up, select your saved path. When you have done this, the default value of 2 is placed in the Flatness box. Enter your value. Now save the file in Photoshop EPS format.

Curved sections of your clipping path are actually made up of straight-line segments. The Flatness value corresponds to the number of straight-line segments that make up a curve. The lower the value, the higher the number of segments. The higher the number of segments, the smoother and more accurate it will be. Values range from .2 to 100. Adobe recommends a value of 8 to 10 for higher resolution images of 1200 to 2400 dpi and 1 to 3 for lower resolution images of 300 to 600 dpi.

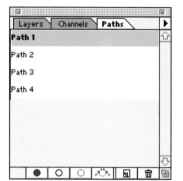

Click once on a path name to select it, twice to change the name.

The Make Selection dialog box.

If you find yourself on a large job with lots of paths to cut, do yourself a favor and pay someone else to do it for you. Making fifty consecutive paths will make your eyes square.

Many people who have no problem making simple paths of all straight segments fall apart when faced with the task of using the curved segments feature of the Pen tool. Like anything else, a little effort applied to learning this skill will get you where you need to go.

Here is a quickie lesson in curved segment paths for intrepid path cutters. The example in the Photoshop manual shows a path beginning and ending on a curve. A more likely scenario is a straight segment path coming up on a curve and then reverting to a straight segment path again. This really only involves two extra keystrokes beyond a straight-line path.

Open up a file of your own and follow along. This path begins with two normal anchor points that are following the straight section. For the third point, set the cursor on the edge of the curved shape, part of the way along its length. To set this point, click and drag. Two handles emerge from this point. The cursor will be on one and there will be a free one. Before you let go of the mouse button, play with the length and angle of the handle until the segment is as close to the curve of the element as possible.

Pulling the handle only a short distance from the anchor point will concentrate the bulk of the curve at the end of the segment near the new anchor point. Pulling the handle out a long way will concentrate the bulk of the curve at the end of the segment nearest the other end. To make a curve that follows a circular shape, such as in the example, pull the handle so that the free handle extends halfway back along the curving segment to the previous anchor point.

Once the curve of the segment is where you want it, click on this last anchor point while holding down the Option key. One of the handles disappears. You are now ready to set the next point. It can be a straight segment or another curve. In my example, I need another curve. To move one of the handles after lifting the mouse button, hold the Command key down. (If the anchor point was not Option-clicked, the next segment curves off to the other side forming an S-curve.)

Start the path as usual, with a straight segment.

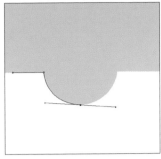

Click and drag when setting the first point of a curve. Before lifting the mouse button, adjust the handles.

The trick to continue from here is to Option-click on the last point. One of the handles will vanish. You can now make another straight-line segment or another curved one.

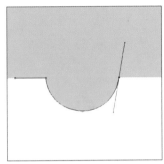

I had to click and drag a second point to finish following the curve. It might have been done with a single click and drag curved segment but the handles would have been extremely long.

Again Option-click on the last point to continue.

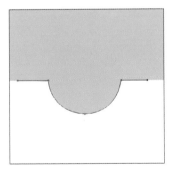

Continue on from this point as per usual.

PART THREE

TECHNICAL AND BUSINESS INFORMATION

Making and enhancing images on the computer is certainly a creative endeavor. I hope you've had a good time looking at the various techniques and components of Photoshop. You will soon discover (if you haven't already) that delving into the digital imaging world demands that you be up to speed on an almost unimaginable amount of technical information. In addition to your photography skills, you must now know quite a bit about prepress in order to achieve a successfully printed conclusion by way of the computer. You'll also need to know about choosing and setting up your system. Take heart. When you do learn these technical skills you will find yourself wiser and empowered— and more marketable to your clients.

In addition to talking about hardware and getting the image out of the computer, this section will cover some of the other useful programs and utilities. I'll end with a brief overview of running a successful digital business.

CHAPTER FIVE

THE SYSTEM
HAVING THE RIGHT HARDWARE

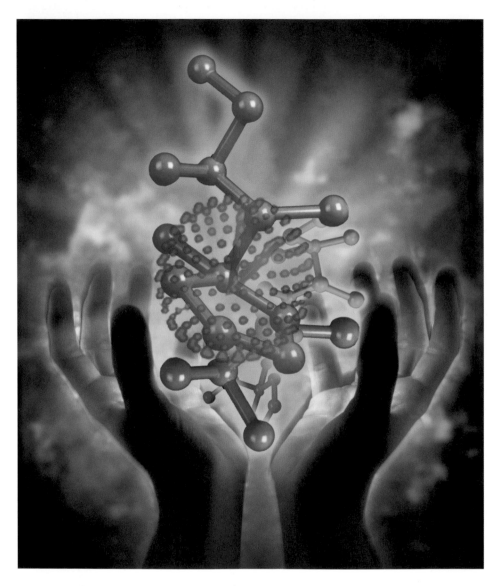

"If automobiles had followed the same development cycle as the computer, a Rolls Royce would today cost a hundred dollars, get a million miles per gallon, and explode once a year, killing everyone inside."

ROBERT CRINGELY

I FIRST HEARD the rumors about electronic photography when I was a photographer's assistant in New York City, close to setting off on my own. "Filmless electronic cameras are being developed and will be in use in just a few years. Digital imagers will use these cameras connected to computers to produce their work." Who were these people? They certainly weren't photographers. None of the shooters I knew or heard of seemed to know any more about these mysterious machines or people than I did. The only thing we were all certain of was that "they" were coming. I was very unnerved by all of this. Here I was, just about to start my career in a medium that I loved, and some wise guys were about to make that medium obsolete. They were going to replace such lovely and tactile things as Plus-X, D-76, Kodachrome, and Nikons with plugs and pixels and CCDs and other soulless stuff.

"They'll still need someone to light the 'merch' and push the button," we said. "If you don't light properly, it doesn't matter what kind of camera you use." We photographers consoled ourselves with thoughts like these but I was still uneasy and angry.

Ironically, the digital camera was feared more than the computer. This was in the early 1980s when desktop computers were just appearing. They seemed like a novelty machine without a purpose. Little did I know.

The anger and trepidation kept me turned off to the idea of going digital for some time. Ten years would pass before I warmed to the idea. In hindsight, this was not an altogether bad thing. It would have been a decade of working with outrageously expensive and painfully slow equipment and software. Those who did do it have my utmost respect.

Those of you who are just now looking for your first machine should consider yourselves lucky. The speed of the machines available today and their relative low cost are big improvements. You'll never have the pleasure of coming back to your computer after an hour to find the little wristwatch still spinning. "If a Radial Blur takes this long on a 6-meg file, how long will it take on a really big file?" I used to ask myself. If you ever stumble across an old Mac IIci or the equivalent with Photoshop on it, don't miss the chance to open a file and play a little. You may be reminded of that first "computer" that took up a whole room and could only add and subtract.

BUYING YOUR FIRST COMPUTER

Your first machine should be the fastest and most powerful you can afford. Don't spend a lot of time fretting about the fact that a faster machine might hit the market six months from now. This has always been true. I have had good luck, when upgrading, by *not* buying the very first computer in a new line. The few bugs that invariably crop up in new computer lines usually get worked out after a few months.

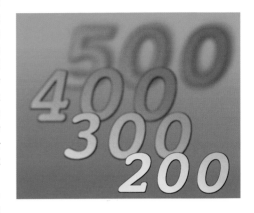

Obsolesence sets in fast. In 1993 I got the impressive new Macintosh Quadra 700. It had 20 megs of RAM and a 230-meg hard drive. It was quite an improvement over my old Mac IIci but it's a dinosaur by today's standards.

Prices are falling while clock speeds are rising. What could be better? My first machine ran at 25 Mhz

Having always worked on a Mac, I don't know much about PCs (though it seems like I may have to learn). PCs have come quite a way, with Windows 95 and Windows NT. There is certainly more software available to PC users. Photoshop does come in a PC version. There are PC cards available for the Mac ($700 to $1000) that allow the Mac user to run PC software.

Most graphic designers and ad agencies are committed to using the Mac and, if you plan to work with any of these people, life will be much simpler if your computer is compatible with theirs. They will need to open your files in their page layout programs and you will probably be asked to work on image files that they have started themselves or obtained elsewhere. Compatibility is a happy thing.

As you buy equipment, put the purchase date, source, and perhaps even the warranty terms on the back or the bottom. This will spare you the miserable job of rooting through all your old receipts from various years trying to sort things out. I learned this from a photographer who dates all his strobe units for the same reason.

Moving around the image and the programs is much easier with an extended keyboard.

MEMORY

I have bad news, good news, and great news for you. I'll give you the bad news first. You'll need RAM and plenty of it. The days when you could get by with 32 megs or less are long gone. Now 48 megs is considered pitiful, 64 megs is an improvement, and 172 megs is only fair. The good news is that memory prices have been dropping rapidly. What started at forty dollars a meg has given way to nine dollars a meg and even less in the magazines and catalogs. The great news is that there are now RAM brokers who quote the price of the chips almost like soybeans and pork bellies. The following address can be used to find the latest prices on the Internet: *www.macresource.com/*. When you get there, look for a button at the bottom of the page called: RAMWATCH. You will come to a page with several vendors and another series of buttons for the various types of chips. Select the button for the chips you need. You will see a screen like the one below.

Make sure that the internal hard drive that comes with your computer is a large one. One to two gigs is fairly standard; four will keep you smiling for a while longer, but get more if you can afford it. One job comprising several layered images and all their supporting elements can easily occupy a gig or more. If you are working on several jobs at the same time you'll be happy about all that extra space.

Most computers come with an extended keyboard these days, though I have seen a few people working on "short" boards (which are very cute and do save space). The extended board has a full complement of F keys across the top as well as Option and Command keys on both sides of the board, not just one. The more you get into Photoshop, the more you will appreciate the shortcuts and the speed keys. Get an extended board.

Prices are currently hovering at around five dollars a meg. Below the prices you'll see about ten company names and phone numbers. I called one of these numbers recently and was quoted a price substantially above the lowest price on the RAMWATCH chart. I said to the guy on the phone, "I'm looking at the RAMWATCH page and I see that someone is selling the chip I want for quite a bit less than you are. I guess I'll have to call around until I find out who it is." "Hang on a second," he said. A hand went over the mouthpiece, papers shuffled around. "Okay, I can match that price for you." It pays to ask.

Only a few years ago 64 megs of RAM cost $2240. That's $35 a meg. Today the same chips would cost about $350. Mark-ups vary greatly. A little searching is worth the effort.

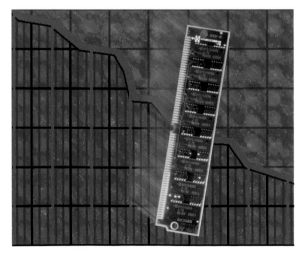

I have not found better prices than those on the Ramwatch page of the Mac Resource Web site.

It's hard to find the image for all the palettes on a small monitor. Treat yourself to large one. You're going to spend a lot of time looking at it.

The new gold standard in removable media are the Zip and Jazz drives by Iomega. The switch from SyQuest was swift.

MONITORS

The bigger your monitor the happier you'll be (especially if you like spending your money). Quality is paramount, though. It is much better to have a 17-inch, high-resolution monitor with a Sony Trinitron tube than some 21-inch "bargain." If you end up with a smaller monitor and Photoshop's palettes are crowding out your image, just hit the tab key to hide them. I have also seen people hook up two monitors to one computer and put all of the palettes on one screen and the image on the other. Buy new. Tubes don't last forever. Colors and brightness fade and the newer monitors have higher resolutions. Magazines like *MacWeek* and *MacUser* are always running in-depth reviews of monitors (if you like lots of technical data, bench tests, and the like).

PORTABLE STORAGE

If you are a photographer you are used to carrying film around and shipping it all over creation. You have a lot more of this in your digital future but files will replace film. Files will need to go to clients, service bureaus, printers, and others. *You* need a portable hard drive. You have many to choose from. The SyQuest system had been the industry standard. It incorporates a single metal platter, identical to the ones in your internal hard drive, although it is a bit slower. Zip and Jazz drives are gaining in popularity very rapidly. They're faster and less expensive than SyQuest drives. I just bought a Zip drive and use it almost exclusively.

If you use a Zip drive, it should be first in the Small Computer System Interface, SCSI (pronounced scuzzy), chain. Otherwise, put your external hard drive first in the chain. Make sure that you turn on all of the SCSI devices and let them spin up to speed and run their self-diagnostics before starting the computer. If the computer locks up part way through the start-up process, the cause of the problem may be a conflict in the SCSI chain. Check all the SCSI ID numbers. I keep a dental hand mirror for just this purpose since my computer is up against a wall. Also check the power cords, one of which may not be seated properly. Internal CD drives are assigned a SCSI number, usually number three, so watch that you don't use this number elsewhere.

For real archiving of your ever-burgeoning pile of elements and images, you need to write the data to Compact Disks. CDR machines use a laser to burn small holes into the reflective coating on a CD. The CD-ROM drive in your computer then reads the alternating holes and reflective patches as ones and zeros. The bottom line here is permanence. Since a CD holds 640 megs, you can save everything that goes into a job—all the elements, all the shots with layers, all the final CMYKs, everything. When your client calls a year later to purchase extended rights but needs a few changes, you just reach for your CD instead of dropping your head into your hands.

The prices for CDR machines have fallen almost as quickly as their speeds have increased. The 2x unit that I paid $1500 for in 1994 could now be replaced with a 6x machine for around $400.

There are other benefits to having a CDR. You can put your portfolio on a CD using one of the many available presentation programs developed for this purpose. They range from the very simple, like Proview 2 from E-magine, to the intimidating, like Macromedia Director.

You can also make a copy of your entire hard drive in anticipation of the day that your computer crashes. You may be the lucky one who never experiences this unique thrill, but for the rest of us, it is a rite of passage. Be ready for your big moment with a copy of all the programs, preferences, extensions, and plug-ins that make up your hard drive.

I once had a poster printed from a digital file that was significantly larger than my 100-meg Zip disk (the 1-gig Jazz drive wasn't available yet). Cutting a CD was a simple and clean solution. There are also programs, like Disk Doubler, that allow you to split large files onto multiple disks, but having the CD ready when reprint time comes around will spare you the trouble of hunting around for multiple disks.

Learning to use the CDR and its software can be a pain. To reduce the stress, make sure that the software that comes with the machine has drag and drop features. Drag and drop allows you to copy files directly from your hard drive or even a removable disk. Files that are to be written to the CD are identified by simply dragging their file or folder icons onto the software's main window. This eliminates the time-consuming practice of having to create partitions and copying all the information destined for the CD into this partition. I use a software package by Toast with great success.

After burning your fifth or sixth CD, the system will probably have paid for itself. I have cut about fifty in the two years I have owned the CDR. At about five dollars a CD, that's cheap storage.

Unless you got a belly whopper of an internal hard drive with your computer, you will eventually need an external hard drive too. Photoshop needs a lot of empty hard drive space to use as scratch disk space or virtual RAM. In fact, it needs more than five times the size of the image file. If you've only got the one drive and it's jam packed with files, then you are asking for trouble in the form of program or system crashes. A second drive will allow you to place all of your files on one drive, and have the System Folder, programs, and a nice clean chunk of empty space on the other. You can then go into the Photoshop preferences, under scratch disks, and tell the program where to look for that empty space first. Of course, an eye-popping amount of RAM would accomplish the same thing and do a better job of it, too. But a second drive will still be necessary

The business side of many recordable CDs has a green cast. Small holes are burned into the reflective surface. The computer reads the holes as ones and the gaps as zeros. The data is not subject to damage from stray magnetic waves the way Zips, SyQuests, and floppies are and the medium is therefore considered archival.

 Don't expect to send in a drive for repair and have any of the data that was on it still be there when it returns. The repair facility will most likely replace the unit. Copy anything you care to keep off to another drive or disk.

if you are pushing any volume of work through your studio.

An internal drive mounted in one of the empty bays would work equally well. They are less expensive and don't take up additional desk space. But there are some advantages to an external drive that you should consider. If you buy a new computer or have more than one on your desk, switching the external drive between machines is a snap. So is sending it in to be repaired. The last drive I bought claimed an MTBF (Mean Time Between Failure) of 800,000 hours. If my math is right, that's about ninety-one years of running twenty-four hours a day, every day of the year. It broke in only ten months. Unplugging it is a lot easier than taking your computer apart to get at an internal drive.

GETTING IMAGES IN: SCANNERS

You'll probably have the most trouble choosing a scanner. The other items are easy by comparison, even the computer itself. With a scanner, though, you really need to know what you need and what to look for.

So what *do* you need? I suppose there are a few people who only work in black and white and therefore only need a gray scale scanner. Most color images that print commercially go to press between 300 dpi and 400 dpi. "Wouldn't a scanner capable of 600 dpi be more than suitable?" you might ask.

Many people, and I grudgingly include myself here, buy their first scanner based on a recommendation or a glowing description in a catalog.

They then struggle with it, learn lots of things they wish they had learned sooner, and eventually go out and buy the scanner that better fits their needs.

Resolution is the most touted and talked about component of a scanner. Dpi is dots per inch, also called ppi or pixels per inch. "This machine has a maximum resolution of X thousand dpi!" the ad blares. "Great, but what is the optical resolution?" should be your response. The CCD chips in the scanner have a specified number of cells that define each pixel. This is the optical resolution. If a scanner has an optical resolution of 600 x 1000 dpi and you tell the machine to scan at 2400 dpi, the scanning software has to interpolate, or invent all those extra pixels. The result is a degradation in sharpness. If the machine had an optical of 2000, you would still be interpolating, but not as much. The hit, or loss, in sharpness would be less severe. You would also find yourself working within the scanner's optical range a higher percentage of the time.

Density range is another important element to look for. This is the range from light to dark that a scanner can hold with detail. The higher the range the more detail the scans will have. A machine with a low-density range will give you muddy, thin blacks (dark grays really), featureless shadows, and blown-out highlights.

A three-pass film or flatbed scanner moves the film or print across its light source or the CCD chip across the material three times, once for each filter—red, green, blue. The color quality from these machines can be better but there is a downside. Not only does the scan take longer than a single-pass scan, but registration can be a problem as well. If the three separate passes don't line up precisely, the result is a thin line of color shift at the top and bottom edge of objects, usually magenta and green. A single-pass machine is not subject to this problem.

I haven't replaced my film scanner with a drum scanner yet although I want to (and I do put one on my Christmas list every year). Occasionally, I have had to scan a high-contrast piece of chrome film twice, once for the highlights and once for the shadows. Then comes the chore of putting the two halves together. I know, I know; I should have just sent out for a decent scan. But the job was due and I didn't want to wait a day. Anyway, I mentioned this problem to a digitally literate, tech-head friend of mine and that's when I first heard about scanning negative film. He intrigued me with the idea of capturing all the information from highlights to shadows in one scan.

In contrasty situations with chrome film, deep shadows tend to block up and highlights are easily blown out. Again, because of the wider dynamic range, negative film will often have the highlight and shadow detail that the chrome film missed. You do need software with your scanner that is able to remove the heavy orange cast. The software that comes with the Agfa Duo scanner has separate curves for many of the more popular negative film bases.

There are a few down sides. Matching color gets *a lot* more subjective without a reference like a transparency. A raw scan from a negative does have a softer look. The blacks aren't quite as intense but Selective Color makes short work of this.

Grain is a problem not so easily dealt with. You can employ 35mm for uses that will never exceed 6 x 9 inches or so. Use 4 x 5 inches for any "large" uses such as a trade show print. The smallest film size I would consider for any size image is 2¼ inches if it may be called upon in the future to go larger. Stock photo usage comes to mind. These parameters are my own, not hard and fast rules. You may like more grain in your images than I do. The people who buy the image as stock may not. I take the conservative route here.

Avoiding the infamous spinning watch is the topic of many digitally oriented conversations.

DIGITAL CAMERAS AND DIGITAL BACKS

Electronic cameras and digital backs are currently very intriguing to me. The lab I use is a ten-minute car ride away. I spend a lot of time running film back and forth and a bunch more scanning it as well. Imagine having your computer on a cart with wheels and just rolling it up to the set. Clip a digital back onto an existing camera, like a Hasselblad, adjust the exposure for brightness and color temperature, and click—you've just saved a ton of time and some money too.

Up to now, digital cameras have been very class-conscious. A camera priced at six hundred to one thousand dollars was good for small newsletters and real estate ads but not much else. Their resolution was low at 640 x 480 dpi. Cameras in the four thousand to ten thousand dollar range implied a midresolution in the neighborhood of perhaps 1000 x 1200 dpi. Everything priced higher was a professional system.

These distinctions are beginning to blur, and as with most computer hardware, these devices are feeling some downward pricing pressure. Great strides are being made in the price, density (resolution), and quality of the CCD chips that are at the heart of the machines.

Some of the 2¼-inch and 4 x 5-inch units employ just a slice of a CCD chip and move it across the image area during exposure. This is called a linear array and can only be used for still objects (provided no one is walking near or bumping into the camera).

Area Array digital cameras and digital backs are more expensive but allow you to capture images at flash-sync speeds. Dicomed, for example, makes a 2¼-inch unit it calls The Big Shot, which has a resolution of 4,096 x 4,096 dpi. It can capture up to 12 bits per color channel, fits certain Hasselblad bodies, and works with strobe lighting, tungsten, HMI, or natural daylight. Some of the big 4 x 5-inch systems can capture 130-megabyte files.

If you gave me a digital back, I'd use it quite a bit, but for the moment I'm still shooting film and scanning. For the type of work that I do, this is just fine. I won't be hampered by a maximum file size. If I get a good piece of film, I know I can get a good scan of any size I may need. Maybe I'm just stubborn. Maybe I don't want to part with thirty thousand dollars. Maybe it's a little of both. There's one in my future, though. I can feel it.

For certain photographers, such as catalog shooters, the pressure is already there to make the switch to a digital camera system. Generally, the smaller and more numerous the pictures in a catalog, the more likely the client will be to ask for digital capability. The attractions for the client are several—money is saved, because all the film, Polaroid, and traditional separation costs are gone, time is saved by not having to run, process, and scan film, and there's the immediate gratification of seeing the image on the screen. The number of clients that are asking for digital just out of curiosity and a desire to try the new medium on for size is increasing as well.

THE IDEAL WORKSTATION

As computers change by getting faster and faster, the perfect environment in which to work changes along with them. My old work area included stacks of magazines, books, and even a small television to keep me occupied while the computer labored endlessly over seemingly simple tasks. Now I don't have time for these distractions.

I love sunshine as much as anyone, yet I spend all of my computer working days in a windowless room. The brightness and color temperature of daylight is much too variable. Your workspace should be equally sunless. Glare on a monitor is also tough to deal with, as you may have already discovered. The room lights should be soft as well. Lights on a dimmer that splash gently on the wall behind the monitor, not on the wall behind you, are what you need. Making subtle corrections to an image demands that your eyes not be tricked or distracted. If the ambient light is too bright, the image may appear too dark when, in fact, it is just right. The inverse is true if the room is too dark. For this same reason, I usually don't work on files in the black screen mode. The images seem brighter because of the dark border and I tend to overdarken them as a result. I like the gray screen mode with the palettes hidden.

Don't waste your hard-earned cash on an antiglare shield. It will only darken the image and you'll probably overcorrect the tonal values as a result. If glare is a problem, you can buy or make a hood that covers the top and the sides of the monitor. Paint the insides a flat black or use black flocking.

Treat yourself to a really nice chair. Splurge—get a leather one. Your rear end is going to be planted in this chair for more hours than you'll want to know about. Whatever kind it is, make sure it gives your back good support.

Floppy disks, Zips, and the like are magnetic media and subject to damage from stray currents, such as the magnetic currents found in speakers and the back end of monitors. Make sure you store your media away from these hazards. CDs are not prone to being corrupted like this but they are not totally impervious either. Keep them clean and free of scratches.

 Rebuild the desktop once a week. Hold the Command and Option keys down together on start up. Occasionally, flaws and kinks begin appearing in the workings of the system software and the application programs. This can often be attributed to problems in the Preferences RAM or PRAM. To reset the PRAM, hold down Command-Option-P-R at start up. After the start-up chimes sound the second time, release the keys. You will notice that little things like the highlight color and the window color are reset to their default settings. On some older machines and Mac OS versions, the memory preferences will reset as well.

 Are you sure you want to rebuild the desktop file on the disk "CU HD"? Comments in info windows will be lost.

Cancel   OK

Rebuilding the desktop once a week will help avoid a myriad of small system errors.

HOT SAUCE
WORKING WITH FIRE

I HAD WANTED to do an image with fire for some time. Several ideas were kicked around, including the one that eventually led to the final sketch below. The shot was originally set outdoors in a field of tall grass in the late afternoon. In the sketch, the grass is burning vigorously. The person in the foreground is cutting the flames fiercely with a scythe while people in the background are harvesting the flames by scooping them up and putting them into vessels of some sort. I was a little concerned about how I was going to show the flames tearing and slicing but, after having overcome larger problems than this in the past, I was confident this one would work out as well. But since it was decided that a more industrial look was necessary, we never got that far.

Once a new composition was settled on, things went very smoothly. With the exception of the windows, which were made more prominent, the final image turned out to be very faithful to the updated sketch.

The models were street recruited. The two guys with the rippling muscles were found in a local gym and were more than willing to be in the picture. Jason Pusey, Mr. Fire there in the foreground (see the final image on pages 110–111), works right in my town and is one of the many locals I call on regularly to pose for me. Each of the three was paid a fee and asked to sign releases.

As much as I like to photograph subjects with light that is as real and accurate as possible, I wasn't about to shoot the models in firelight. I did make a large fire to shoot but the models

The final sketch.

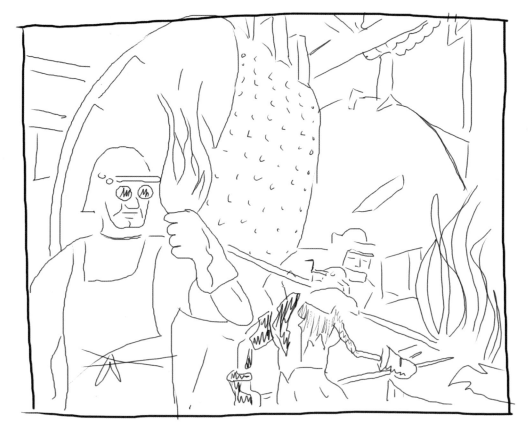

were kept in the studio. A combination of orange and yellow gels in light banks did the trick.

Morris Minis with little slices of the same "fire" gels were used to light the inside of the bucket in the lower left and the underside of the raised glove on Jason. The fire was then placed on top of the glow.

Morris Minis are small flash units about the size of a deck of cards. They're powered by AAA batteries and have tiny electric eyes that trigger off of any other flash, allowing you to put them almost anywhere. I hear newspaper photographers tape hat pins to them, and stick the units into the ceiling for a top or a back light. At about twenty-five dollars a unit, anyone can afford to toss a few into his or her kit.

For the model's eyewear, several styles of goggles were ordered from a safety equipment catalog. Jason's apron was borrowed from a friend who dabbles in blacksmithing, and the gloves are old bee-keepers gloves that I found in an antiques store.

During the time that the foreground elements were being photographed, I was on the prowl for industrial interiors that would net me a set of high windows with tons of sun streaming in and a large expanse of floor. Ideally, the room would be a little dusty so the rays of sun would really

The two fire tenders above were shot in the studio with warm gels to the right and cool ones to the left. With large windows destined to appear above them, a bright backlight was also added.

The raised hand on the model at left was eventually reshot when it was decided that flames were needed on the bottom of the hand.

show. Finding a long row of windows was not, as it turned out, too difficult. I found exactly what I needed in a factory building right in my town. Unfortunately, they faced north and were very low to the floor. I shot them anyway from only inches off the ground. If a better situation didn't turn up, I would at least have these. Finding an uncluttered factory floor and getting permission to shoot it were turning out to be more challenging feats.

Between searches, I began making a temporary interior right in the computer, just so the elements could be placed and evaluated. The image began taking shape. Laziness being the true mother of invention, I began to think that with a little fine-tuning and a healthy dose of Gaussian Blur, my fake factory (built around the real windows) might have possibilities. Here is what I did.

With the figures placed in the foreground, the background was filled with a dark, charcoal gray. The Line tool was then used to arrive at the correct angle for where the floor and wall meet. With the floor defined, it was selected and filled with a lighter gray.

The windows were dropped in next. My low camera angle was not low enough and quite a bit of twisting and stretching took place with the help of the Free Transform tool. The bluish cast of the original file was retained as it looked good against the warm foreground tones. A single back window was created in a separate file using the Marquee and Paint Bucket tools. Once it was pasted into the main image, it was copied multiple times by first selecting it with the Marquee tool and then clicking and dragging with the Command and Option keys held down. The small size of the windows helped create the feeling of a cavernous space.

I liked these windows but they were not high enough to get the proper perspective.

I tried to create the feeling of sun pouring into the space with one big, feathered selection but it didn't look right. Even cutting slices into it to imply separate rays from each window didn't work. I finally realized that I had to make the rays for each window individually and let them overlap. Each selection was feathered to about 25 pixels and filled with about 20 percent pure white. The overlaps became brighter, creating an additive effect. This all took place on a new layer. The Create New Layer command is one I use often and have an F key assigned to it.

The final ingredient to the sunlight effect was the floor. The parts of the floor under these new rays of sun needed to be brightened. I selected them with a Lasso set to 0 instead of a feathered

After extending the windows, the Free Transform tool was used to twist them into the correct perspective. The ones along the back wall were painted in.

To arrive at a realistic look, the rays of light were built up one at a time. Each selection was filled with white at 10 percent opacity.

The rays of light ended up becoming a very important element, as evidenced by this version without them.

one so that I could control the amount of blur later using Gaussian Blur. The selections were made on the charcoal black background layer and brightened with Curves.

The room still looked a little sparse so a few details were added to make the place seem more plausible. A small slice of an industrial ceiling was taken from a file shot as were the shapes under the windows. These elements were both forced into the correct perspective with the help of the Free Transform tool. I reach for this tool so often that hitting Command-T seems like too much work. It's tagged to another F key.

Now I wanted to add some visual interest by blurring all the elements behind the three guys. I didn't want a straight blur, however. It was to be a progressive blur, starting weakly just behind the figures and getting stronger the farther back into the room it went. As in the previous image description, Quick Mask was used with the Gradient tool set to Linear to produce a soft, left to right, gradated selection. The Gaussian Blur filter

was then run through the selection, resulting in a graduated blur. (This technique was described more fully in the Jet Lighter and Alpha Channels sections, Part One.) All the layers behind the models were chosen and, without changing the selection, the filter was applied to each.

The blur was pleasing, but I wanted to take it a little further. The figure of Jason was on its own layer. I made a duplicate of this layer and placed it behind (under) the original. This dupe layer was then given a Gaussian Blur of about 20 pixels. The effect of this blur shows up mainly behind Jason's lowered arm and shoulder. In fact, I partially erased away the edge of his arm to accentuate the effect. A soft Eraser with the opacity set to 25 percent was used.

The flames and smoke were selected from their original files with Color Range. The resulting selection was then feathered and copied. After deleting the entire file to white, the copied selection was pasted back in. Unwanted parts that were inadvertently selected got removed.

Color Range was used to select the smoke and flames. This selection was pasted to its own layer. With the flames on a separate layer, coming back to this element over and over again to select small areas is easy.

With the cleaned up fire on its own layer, I was able to easily grab bits and pieces with a simple Lasso. These pieces were copied, pasted into the final, and merged into their own single layer. On top of this layer was the Glow layer. The Airbrush was set to about 8 percent opacity and was used to brush on a very light yellow, almost white. This made the fire look much more alive and vibrant.

The bottle of "Hot Sauce" was photographed with a gold foil card behind it. Since we had planned to put some fire on the surface of the liquid, the bulk of the effect of this card was aimed here.

Both the table and the bottle were shot from several tripod heights so that I would be sure to have one that fit the perspective. Had I remembered to mark the height and placement of the tripod as I usually do, it wouldn't have been necessary.

Through all of this, the windows were left showing the featureless white they were shot with. Although I liked this, the value of the white competed with the fire. The sunset brought the value down and also gave the warm foreground elements something to play off of. Of course, the shafts of light no longer made perfect sense. But I liked them too much to take them out.

The window panes were selected with Color Range and the Paste Into command was used to bring in the sunset. A Gaussian Blur helped it match the focus of the image.

The bottle was backlit in anticipation of adding some fire to the liquid's surface. The odd surface under the bottle came from the spray booth of a cabinetmaker's shop.

The last thing to do was to put some sort of floor under the two guys poking at the pot of fire. A separate layer was made and the lower right corner was filled with what I intended to be the lightest value. A huge Eraser was used to soften the edges. The same gradated Quick Mask technique as above was used to make a selection, except the Gradient tool was set to Radial instead of Linear. With this selection and Curves, I darkened the floor progressively away from the fire. A small amount of Noise was added to the floor and a small Gaussian Blur of .5 pixels blended the Noise in a bit.

A feathered Lasso made the selections that were used to make the shadows of the guys' legs on the floor. These shadows were made on their own layer in case the figures were ever moved. A dark brown filled the selections and then the layer opacity was pulled down to 55 percent. A large, soft Eraser removed some of the left side of the shadow, making it look weaker farther away from the legs.

Generally, I am pleased with the image. As with most shots, I see things that I would like to improve further—if only time allowed. The perspective relationship between the two guys, Jason, and the floor doesn't quite seem right, for example. But despite its shortcomings, I like the image.

The final image.

CHAPTER SIX

HOW DO I GET THE PICTURE OUT?

FROM PIXELS TO PRESS

"A ship in the harbor is safe. But that's not what ships are built for."

ANONYMOUS

T SEEMS LIKE most people are more or less self-taught when it comes to imaging. They may buy books like this one or take short seminars, but the bulk of what they know comes from playing with the programs, working on actual projects, suffering through a few disasters, and calling Photoshop-literate friends for advice.

For these people, there will be three basic phases to their imaging scholarship. The first phase involves groping around and learning the programs. The second phase starts as they become a little comfortable and perhaps even intoxicated with the power at their disposal. The third phase begins the day they bring home their first unhappy four-color proof. On this day they realize that perhaps learning more about separations, inks, and calibration might be worth the effort after all.

Since computers ultimately understand only 1s and 0s, you would think that there would be a very precise and direct way of moving your images from disk to print. "Set these values to X, choose this button, make sure there is exactly X amount of magenta in the fleshtones," and so on. The reality is something else. There is still a lot of room for human impact at every stage of the process. Two printers may have the same model presses but because of the way they maintain and run them, the same file printed on each would look different. One of my clients, who goes on press himself, really likes to lay a lot of ink on paper. I have to take this into account when preparing files. Someone else printing the same file would likely arrive at a different end result. The process is still very much something of an art form and it takes experience and a little touch of artistry to work it out.

CALIBRATION

Getting the image on the screen out correctly presumes it is being viewed correctly. If the monitor and Color Preferences are not set properly, many surprises await. We're talking about calibration here. Since calibration can be described as bringing a device exactly in line with a known reference, true calibration requires that we enter these reference values for all our input and output devices. The values we plug into the Color Preferences windows are specific enough. This is not as much fun as playing with a plug-in filter but it is very necessary. Let's start with the Monitor Setup dialog box.

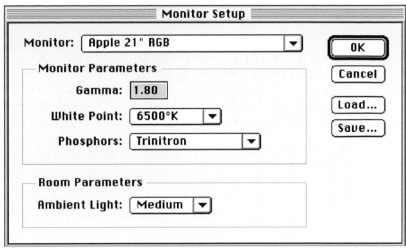

Completing the Monitor Setup dialog box is important. The way Photoshop displays the image is partly controlled by the settings here. Unlike the other color preferences setups, this one is "set it and forget it."

Under File in the menu, go down to Color Settings and over to Monitor Setup. Next to Monitor, find your monitor (or one whose characteristics are close to yours) in the pop-down menu of names. For Gamma, choose 1.8 for print work and 2.2 for electronic uses like multimedia and video.

For White Point, 5000k is the standard in the U.S. while 6500k seems to be the standard elsewhere in the world. If you found your monitor, or one you know is similar, in the first list, leave the Phosphors setting alone. If you didn't find a good match and chose Other, get the correct x, y settings from the manufacturer, choose Custom, and plug them in.

As I mentioned in the previous chapter, the ambient light in your work area should be consistent, glare free, and a bit lower than the screen brightness. Choose Low from Ambient Light if it is. Choose Medium if the values match, and High if the room light is brighter (hopefully not). Save these settings with the save button in the dialog box.

How do you handle the monitor itself, which may have only a few dials with no correlation to any specific number values? They also get dimmer as they age. The only way that results in true calibration requires the use of expensive hardware calibration systems. The instructions for using them vary with each unit so I'll limit the description to the method you have access to right now, using the Gamma control.

Adjusting your monitor with Gamma is more of an eyeball experience and doesn't really represent true calibration. Many photographers and small shops get by with it all the same.

Working with the Gamma dialog box involves a little back and forth between its various controls and the monitors. What will happen is that you will get the monitor set as close as possible, save the settings as a baseline standard, and then once you begin using output devices, separate Gamma settings will be made (if necessary) and saved for each output device you use.

Make sure the monitor has warmed up for at least a half hour and that the ambient light in the room is in the condition that you will do all of your work. Open the Carmen Miranda image that comes with Photoshop. They call it "Ole No Moire." Set the controls on the monitor to give the image pleasing brightness and contrast. Close the image. Put tape over the controls and don't change them. If these controls are dials, mark them before taping.

Place the Gamma icon, found in Photoshop's Calibration folder, into the Apple menu items. Launch Photoshop and create a new file. Fill this file with a completely neutral, middle gray. To get this gray, open the Color Picker and slide the circular cursor all the way over to the left and about halfway up the side. Set the screen to full screen mode, zoom into the image, and hide the palettes by hitting the Tab key.

Launch Gamma from the Apple menu items. Check the buttons at the lower left to make sure it's on. Choose the same target Gamma as was done in the Monitors Setup. For me that would be 1.8. Next, drag the Gamma adjustment slider a little left or right to make the solid gray bars match

the textured ones. This won't be far if the monitor controls are set right. If it is far, you will want to adjust those monitor controls and begin again.

The next step is to set the White Point. Check its radio button. Hold a piece of white paper next to the monitor while doing this. It needs to be illuminated by correct light such as daylight-rated fluorescent tubes. Now drag the three sliders until the white in the monitor is the same as the paper. Most monitors have a bluish cast so start with the blue slider.

After clicking the Balance radio button, remove any color cast in the band of gray below the sliders by adjusting its sliders.

The last button is for the Black Point adjustment. Move its sliders until there is no color cast in the shadow end of the gray band below the sliders.

As the sliders are being moved around, you'll notice that the changes made with one set affect the others. You'll need to go back and forth, making ever smaller changes, until they all agree. Bring Carmen Miranda back to the screen and make sure that the brightness and contrast settings still look good. Now save the Gamma settings and label it "baseline" or some such.

THE FIRST MATCH PRINT

So your match print or film output came back and it doesn't look like the screen. Now what do you do? You make the image on the screen look as much like the print or film as possible, correct the image again, and make a new match print. When you first adjusted the monitor, you changed the Gamma settings to compensate for any color casts it had. The match print is telling you that your "corrected" monitor is not in sync with that particular service bureau or printer. What you are going to do is to create a Gamma Curve for that service bureau or printer and save it. Here's how.

Make sure the screen has been on and warming up for at least a half hour and that the room lighting is optimal. Open the Gamma dialog box and turn Gamma on if it isn't already (it should be). Start with the Gamma Adjustment slider. If the image is too light or dark, make the adjustment here. Since your monitor has already been adjusted, the values should be close. If not, something is wrong. Check through all the possibilities such as Monitor Setup, the brightness/ contrast dials on the monitor itself, and so on. Check with the printer next. They're not infalli-

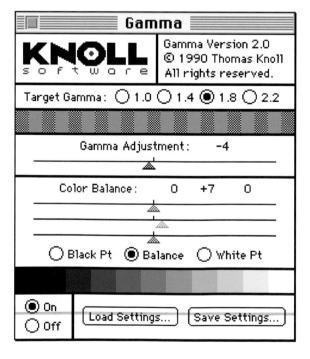

ble. I once had a set of match prints come back that were very chalky and desaturated. The printer eventually tracked down the error to a problem on their end but not before I spent a rough day and a half worrying about it.

For the color adjustment, use only the Balance radio button in the center. The amount of correction needed to eliminate a slight color cast won't be much. Move the red, green, and blue sliders in small increments. Overcorrecting will not help you in the least. Save this Gamma setting with a name that identifies the printer.

Now the image looks "wrong" again. Make the necessary corrections in Photoshop to bring it visually back "right" and make a new match print.

This new Gamma Curve will not replace your baseline settings. Instead, it will be saved separately and loaded each time you are working on images that are destined to go through that service bureau or printer again. Unless you are very lucky, almost every output device you use will need a separate curve.

SETUP CONSIDERATIONS

Before going into four-color considerations, there are a few types of output that only require an RGB file or three colors. Film recorders such as the LVT and Fire 1000 make transparencies from digital files. The Fire 1000 has a resolution of 1270 dpi but files can be run at about half of that. The minimum resolution for a 4 x 5 inch file destined for this machine is 600 dpi. Because I make 4 x 5 inch chromes of the images that will go into the portfolio or into stock, I build these files at this resolution.

Some digital prints can also be rendered from an RGB file. Dye-subs and Fijix are two examples. The dye-sub machines can also be run with a four-color ribbon and used as color proofers. Kodak makes the 8650 and the 9000—8½ x 11 inch and 11 x 17 inch respectively. Epson also makes a series of inexpensive printers that, while not all reliable as accurate proofers, are terrific for showing comps and progress sketches. Starting at three hundred dollars, they're hard to pass up.

Most color work in Photoshop is done in the color mode called RGB even though the end product may eventually need to be CMYK. RGB files, having the three channels of red, green, and blue, are smaller than CMYK files with their four channels of cyan, magenta, yellow, and black. As smaller files, they open faster, work faster, and take up less space. So why not just

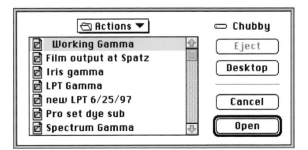

Make and save a Gamma Curve for each printer or output device that needs one.

have the commercial printers use the RGB files to print from instead of going through the pain of converting them all to CMYK? Imaging life would be so much simpler if only that were possible.

Printers can't use red, green, and blue ink and show all the colors that we expect. How would they show black? Your RGB file displayed on your RGB monitor can show black by holding back light, but the printed image relies on reflected light. To show a deep black you need black ink. And to show all the tints of each color, black ink must be added to C, M, and Y in varying amounts.

Below are two images. The first has been converted to CMYK. The second is the same image with the black channel turned off. To go to press, we need the black channel and therefore we need to convert our files to CMYK.

A CMYK image with all its channels intact.

The same image without the black channel.

The formula by which a program like Photoshop converts a file into CMYK is not a constant. During the process information is retrieved from three places: the Monitor Setup, the Printing Inks Setup, and the Separation Setup dialog boxes. The last two need to be changed for each job if the output device is different. If you prepare your files for a brochure that is to be printed on coated paper and then hand the same files to people who hope to print the images on newsprint, they'll have a problem on their hands.

The Printing Inks dialog box is where the qualities of the paper and ink you will be printing with are defined. The output device, Dot Gain, and Gray Balance settings comprise the controls. The Printing Inks Setup also plays a role in the way your CMYK file appears on the screen. Your monitor is an RGB device. When a file is converted to CMYK, the underlying data has changed but the image on the screen is actually an RGB approximation of a CMYK. Some of the information Photoshop uses to display an accurate representation of this CMYK comes from the Printing Inks Setup.

The first step is to select an ink type or a specific device. When it comes time to go to press, you will have many questions for the printer. The first one can be about which ink color preset to use. In the U.S., one of the SWOP (Specs for Web Offset Printing) presets such as the SWOP Coated will likely be the choice. When one is chosen, a default Dot Gain setting is automatically entered. Leave this default Dot Gain alone until the first proof comes back unless the printer tells you otherwise.

The term "dot gain" refers to the increase in size of the ink halftone dots when going from film to press. The ink spreads as it touches the

Although this is just a filter-generated re-creation of the printed page, you can see that if each dot were to spread larger than anticipated, the image would be darker if not muddier.

paper. Different papers have variable absorption rates and therefore higher or lower dot gain amounts. If the halftone dots were to spread more or less than anticipated, the brightness and contrast of the image would be altered. An increase would darken and perhaps muddy the image while a decrease would leave the image looking light and chalky.

The amount of dot gain is determined by a densitometer reading of the match print or printed piece. A 50 percent halftone dot that reads as 65 percent will be said to have a 15 percent dot gain. In this instance, 15 percent is the number you want in the Printing Inks Dot Gain window. If you find yourself wanting to change this value as a result of looking at the proof, remember that simply changing the number won't affect the CMYK file. You will need to go back to the RGB file and reseparate with the new value.

GENERATING THE BLACK PLATE

To better understand the way the Separation Setup preferences work, it is helpful to know the difference between Additive and Subtractive colors. When looking at an image on the monitor or even at a television, you are looking at additive colors. These are RGB devices. Everything you see is generated from red, green, and blue. Even the visual representation of a CMYK file on the screen is being approximated by red, green, and blue. These colors begin with a light source. They are additive because the more color you add, the lighter or closer to white things become. Holding back all color creates black.

The Printing Inks Setup needs to be set for each individual job.

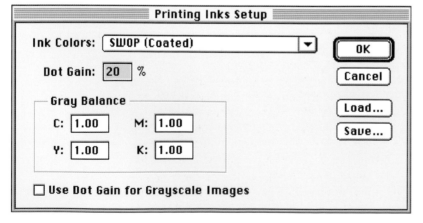

Printing Inks Setup

Ink Colors: SWOP (Coated) ▼   OK

Dot Gain: 20 %   Cancel

Gray Balance
C: 1.00   M: 1.00   Load...
Y: 1.00   K: 1.00   Save...

☐ Use Dot Gain for Grayscale Images

A printed image cannot beam light through itself. It must rely on light bouncing off the surface of the inks. Subtracting ink reveals the white paper and the image appears lighter or closer to white. Adding ink causes parts of the light spectrum to be absorbed depending on the percentages of ink used. The image gets darker. The three primary ink colors are cyan, magenta, and yellow. In a perfect world, enough of these colors could be mixed together to produce black but impurities in the inks prevent this from being possible. A dark, brownish-gray is the result instead. Replacing these muddy areas with black ink overcomes this problem. Since three inks are replaced with one, less ink is used in the bargain.

There is more than one way to generate this fourth, or black plate. The Separation Setup dialog box allows you to determine which method to use and to quantify the process. The two methods, GCR and UCR, are found next to Separation type. UCR stands for Undercolor Removal. Separations made with UCR remove some of the three inks, C, M, and Y, from the neutral areas and replace them with black. Other areas are comprised of C, M, and Y only. The result is more ink in these areas and less ink in the shadow areas.

GCR stands for Gray Component Replacement. GCR seps also replace neutral or gray component areas with black ink but the blacks extend a little further into the nonneutral color areas as well. Less ink is necessary to reproduce these areas.

If GCR is chosen, the Black Generation pop-up makes itself available. The choice selected determines the strength of the black generation. Light, Medium, and Maximum replace increasingly wider portions of the tonal range with black. Light or Medium is the place to start. Medium is the default setting. Selecting None causes no neutrals to be replaced by black, a separation with basically no black plate at all. GCR Setup values can vary quite a lot depending on the image that is being separated. A collage piece may need widely different settings from a straight portrait shot. Before converting to CMYK, consult with your printer or service bureau to get more specific values to use as a starting point.

The theoretical ink limit is 400 percent, 100 percent of each of C, M, Y, and K. This would probably make a soggy mess when printed on paper so limiting the total ink becomes necessary. The default is 300 percent but I find that 310 to 320 percent, for coated stock, works well for

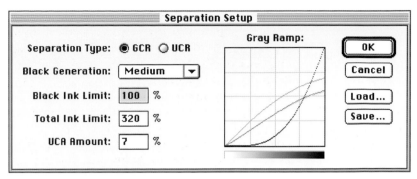

me. I leave the Black Ink Limit at its default of 100 percent, and set the UCA amount to 5 percent.

The last setting in the Separation Setup window is UCA. UCA stands for Undercolor Addition and is only available when GCR is the chosen sep type. Since GCR uses more black over a broader range of colors, it is possible for shadows to sometimes appear a bit lifeless. UCA adds some C, M, and Y back in these areas and, therefore, gives it a little more depth and life. I add 5 percent.

Virtually all of the print work I do is destined for coated stock and the numbers I have given here are reflective of that. Check with your printer for other papers, such as uncoated stocks.

These dialog boxes only affect images that are converted "through" them. Merely making changes to the settings doesn't change the data in any existing file. If you have already made a file CMYK and then decide to alter any of the setups, the file must be reconverted. Hopefully, this means that you will open the RGB that you saved prior to making the first CMYK, and convert *it*. Changing a CMYK file to RGB and then back to CMYK through your new settings would also work, but since a lot of information is lost at each mode change, it is not the preferable way. Save CMYK files separately from RGBs.

COLOR GAMUTS

Because black is added to the other inks of cyan, magenta, and yellow to arrive at the various tints, and because of impurities in the inks, CMYK files cannot show all the colors that are possible in RGB. RGB files are able to display some extremely fluorescent hues. Trying to convert one of these files to CMYK and hoping that no color is lost is like trying to pound a three-inch peg through a two-inch hole without some wood coming off—impossible. The colors that are out of reach of CMYK are considered to be out of gamut.

Taken one at a time, the individual aspects of the Separation Setup dialog box are not too difficult to grasp.

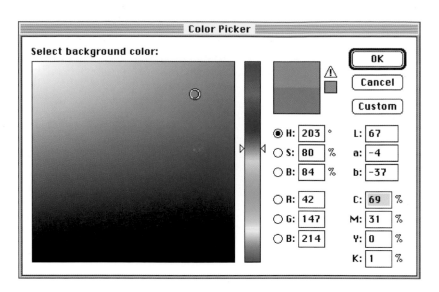

Look for the exclamation point next to the OK in the Color Picker. When present, it tells you that the selected color is out of Gamut.

If you have ever converted an image to CMYK and witnessed a large change in the appearance, then you had several areas of out-of-gamut, RGB colors that were squeezed back *into* CMYK gamut colors during the conversion. Bright blues, purples, and reds are among the first to suffer and appear duller and flatter in a converted image.

Is it possible to tell if a color is out of gamut early on so as to avoid last-minute surprises? Absolutely. There are four ways.

Sample a Color from Your Image with the Eyedropper

Click on that color in the Foreground color box in the Toolbox and the Picker comes up. If the triangular box with the exclamation point inside is displayed in the upper right, your color is out of gamut.

With an RGB Image on the Screen, Hit Command-Y

This is the CMYK Preview command. Photoshop does a quick approximation of your image as a CMYK. This is only a preview. Your file is still RGB. Clicking in and out of CMYK Preview will help you locate the trouble spots. This command can also be found in the View column of the menu bar.

Turn on Gamut Warning

This is a more accurate way of seeing all the out-of-gamut areas. This will cover every out-of-gamut pixel with a bright color that you choose in Gamut Warning Preferences.

Develop Experience with CMYK Files

Once you have gained some experience with CMYK files you will find yourself recognizing problem colors well before reaching for CMYK Preview or Gamut Warning. Your RGB images will need less and less radical adjustment as time goes by. Using the above methods are always a good idea, however.

IN SUMMARY

The Color Preferences act like a filter of sorts, constraining the parameters of your RGB files during the conversion process. Once the file is a CMYK, however, there are no constraints. Any corrections made are bounded by nothing and could push numbers such as Total Ink beyond your working tolerances. Ideally, any changes made to the CMYK file are done only while viewing a match print. If you are consistently making large moves at this point, the Color Prefs should be updated.

Viewing match prints under anything but color-corrected light is a mistake and a waste of your time. Small light booths can be purchased or you can make your own with daylight-rated fluorescent tubes.

By now, you may be getting a sense of increased responsibility as a result—handing over a file that you've just converted to CMYK. If someone else such as a graphic designer or ad agency is handling the printing, you will either need to get the printing information from them, get in touch with the printer directly, get your scans and do all of your work in CMYK, or hand your clients an RGB file and let them do the

CMYK conversion themselves. This last option is certainly the easiest but not necessarily the safest. You could be handing the file off to someone who knows even less about the process than you do. That person may simply convert to CMYK with Photoshop's default settings, go whistling off to the printer, and still come back to you if things go sour. Take pains to clarify your responsibilities at this critical juncture.

I have seen a few people attempt to learn about output while executing a job. This is like trying to learn tight-rope walking while the rope is thirty feet in the air. You won't get killed when you fall but it will hurt. The pain, in this case, will come in the form of agitated phone calls from your clients (not fun) and perhaps the cost of extra match prints. Take steps to avoid this. Devote the time to move a sample image from the raw scans to a reliable output such as a match print. A printer who thinks you will be bringing in respectable amounts of work may give you a discount on the prints. If these sorts of steps are taken, your palms won't get nearly so sweaty at press time.

Gamut Warning

Color: [ ] **Opacity:** 85 %

The Gamut Warning preferences are user-set with the color and opacity of your choice.

An image may seem okay, but checking for colors that are out of gamut may reveal that they are not. The Gamut Warning from View in the main menu gives a visual reference to out-of-gamut areas (right).

CHAPTER SEVEN

GET WITH THE PROGRAMS

EXCITING SUPPLEMENTAL SOFTWARE

"Luck is what happens when preparation meets opportunity."

DARREL ROYAL

T TAKES MORE than a page layout program to make you a designer and more than a copy of Photoshop to make you a digital photographer. The ready availability of computers and programs, however, is causing some to try and perform more of the work they used to hire out. Designers and ad people are doing image retouching and separation work. Photographers are doing page layout and publishing work. I won't try to tell you what to do. If you can wear a few different hats, handle all the programs, and still keep your business running smoothly, God bless you. I've seen what good designers do— I'm sticking to photography.

The following program descriptions represent only a handful of the many that are available. A quick spin through any of the computer catalogs clogging your mailbox will show you that. These, though, are my favorites. Some are as comprehensive as Photoshop and a few are quite small—utilities really.

LIVE PICTURE: RESOLUTION-INDEPENDENT IMAGING

I am just now getting to know Live Picture. It is a stunning piece of software. The company that

developed it is touting it as the next gold standard for image editing. It is not hard to see why.

Imagine working on an image that is destined to be a 30 x 40-inch trade-show print. In Photoshop, that's 309 megs (RGB) before you even touch it. You are rotating layers, color correcting, making drop shadows, and generally doing all sorts of manipulation. Now picture all this work happening in real time. There are no little spinning clock hands or progress bars. Commands are executed almost as fast as you can push the buttons. You can undo or partially undo one command, a few commands, or all of them, all the way back to the beginning. Your ability to undo is unlimited. You can even do this without truckloads of RAM. How can this be?

There are two secrets to this revolutionary program. They are file formats called IVUE and FITS. IVUE files are pixel based, just as Photoshop files are. Instead of having just one resolution of, say, 600 dpi, IVUE images have this resolution plus a whole series of lower-resolution images as well. These smaller images contain just enough data to fill the screen as you work. Since your monitor most likely has a physical resolution of only 72 dpi, these images are small

Imported as IVUE files, images and elements can be viewed in many different cropping windows. Since the building process does not alter the elements it reads from, any of the views can be built at any time.

indeed. Live Picture never needs to load the entire file into memory the way Photoshop does. This is a big time saver. A 450-meg image would load just as quickly as a 1-meg file. Files can be scanned into this format or converted easily from other formats, both in Live Picture directly or with a purpose-built utility that comes with it.

FITS, which stands for Functional Interpolation Transformational System, is the file format or workspace that you see as you are manipulating the image. It retrieves the appropriate image from the IVUE file depending on how far you have zoomed into the image. Some people are under the mistaken notion that these are proxy images. If you zoomed into a proxy image, it would quickly become very pixelated looking. As you magnify a Live Picture image, a new sub-image from the IVUE file is loaded so that you always have a crisp, sharp view. This is why FITS is referred to as a resolution-independent format.

Each change or adjustment is stored as a mathematical description. These descriptions are used to build the final image. When the Build command is used, a new image is constructed. The source or IVUE files themselves are never altered. The size of a final image (without interpolation) is limited only by the size of the source elements.

Live Picture does not claim to be everything that Photoshop is. Its creators expect users of Live Picture also to have Photoshop, or an equivalent, so that the two can work hand in hand. Most complex elements opened in Live Picture should first be "washed" through Photoshop. If

these two programs could ever be rolled into one, that would be something to behold.

Live Picture does go head to head with Photoshop in silhouetting, though, and it wins. In fact, when an element is opened in Live Picture for this purpose, it comes in on a special silhouetting layer complete with its own set of tools. For elements that have hard edges and are already on a fairly clean background, the process is very quick. For trickier silos, such as a head shot of a person with fuzzy hair, it gets more involved, but Photoshop can't compare to what Live Picture does in these situations.

BRYCE

Caution. Bryce, by MetaCreations, is dangerous. You may become addicted after only a few doses. If you are trying to cut back your use of fun and useful programs, don't dabble with this one.

With Bryce, you can play God by creating mountains, oceans, deserts, trees, and so on. You have the power to manipulate sunlight (or moonlight), clouds, haze, and fog. Cubes, spheres, and artificial light sources will do what you want them to do. You can assign them any of the hundreds of available textures. Each of these textures can also be customized almost infinitely. Since PICT files that you create can be brought in and applied to the surface qualities of any object, perhaps the possibilities *are* infinite. Objects can be grouped together and then moved around the scene as a single object.

The only drawback is that to get the dreamy qualities of light and color that Bryce gets, it must use ray-tracing. Ray-tracing is a programming scheme that calculates the value of each pixel, taking into account the apparent distance into the background, the color and angle of the light, the amount and height of any haze or fog, and so on. It does the job well, but it can be very

The Build dialog box awaits your instructions as to dimensions and resolution. The only requirement is that the elements be large enough to support the largest build size or Live Picture will have to interpolate.

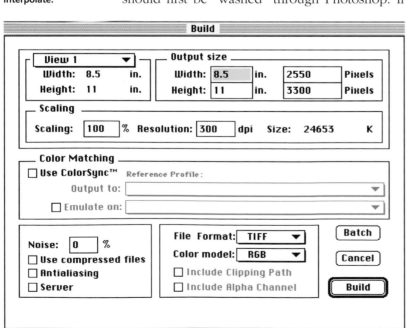

If you've been playing with computers for a while, you probably have more than one at your disposal. Why not let your slower computer chomp away at Bryce instead of just collecting dust or sitting there tied to a printer? This is the best way to fine-tune a Bryce background while you are editing foreground elements in Photoshop or Live Picture.

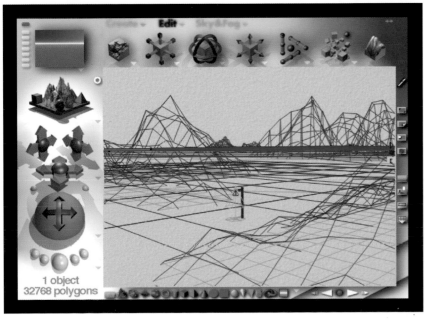

Bryce landscapes are striking. As stand-alones, you won't fool too many people into thinking they're photos. But if you put them in the background, apply a Gaussian Blur, and put the real element in the foreground, you might have something.

Left, the Bryce desktop is practically language free. It's one of those programs that almost needs no manual.

One of the interesting features of Bryce is the ability it has to blend PICT files with objects. In this example, the PICT was blended with a mountain. The blend amount was 100 percent so none of the surrounding mountain remains.

Light sources and geometric shapes can also be created.

slow on older machines. A complicated, high-resolution file might take many hours to complete depending on the final resolution of the image and which computer it is being rendered on.

The programmers of Bryce were very sensitive to this. There are a few ways in which to preview the final image. My favorite way lets you select any rectangular piece of the image and render it to completion. Another way is to choose Preview mode. This mode renders all of the objects in a uniform gray, allowing you to see at least the transition from wire frame to solid. There is also a small color preview window in the upper left of the screen.

PAINTER

I originally got Painter, another MetaCreations offering, to achieve an illustrative look for a project I was working on. (A full description of this particular technique can be found in the section Boy with Bell, page 133.) In the process, I discovered a great program with real depth. With all of its paint and surface-control attributes, Painter is a natural for illustrators and the like. But since it can open TIFFs and Photoshop files, including ones with layers and paths, it can also be useful to photographers and digital artists looking for new looks. I've always liked to paint and draw, so this program is a real hoot just to play with.

I originally got Painter to produce a series of images needed for an assignment. Discovering a deep and versatile program with many other useful applications was a bonus.

The original photo of Stromness. This is the first view of the Orkney Islands as seen from the morning ferry off mainland Scotland.

Colors taken directly from the image are saved in a new Color Set. These new sets become part of the permanent library. The colors can then be applied to the image with any of the many tools and variants.

For the image above, I opened a picture I had taken of the Orkney Islands, Scotland, as a TIFF. What I wanted to achieve was a pastel-like rendering of the photograph. A color set was made by sampling colors directly from the photo. These colors would then be used when applying the chalk.

The next step was to apply a surface texture directly to the photo. This texture is completely controllable—from the size and the color to the direction and the color of the light that defines it. The textures in Painter simulate rough papers, with various grains, so the Chalk brush in Painter has some "tooth" to grab onto. At the same time, some of the photo shows through between the ridges so that the end product is actually a composite of a drawing and a photo.

Even though you can set Painter to perform up to 32 consecutive undos (think about that), the file was saved so that I could experiment with different brush qualities. Once all the various brush attributes were set, the brush profile itself was saved so that I could go back to it easily. Colors were taken from the new Color Set

and brushed onto the photo. I eventually wanted some colors that weren't in the original picture so I went to the color wheel in the Art Materials palette to select them.

Another way to render a photograph is to first check its pixel dimensions and then open a "sheet of paper" of the same size. Now place the photo on top of the paper as a floater (Painter's term for layer). Reduce the opacity of the floater so that you can still see it but also still see what the paintbrushes are doing. Now use all of Painter's various brushes and "mediums" to render the image like an electronic paint-by-numbers. When you are done, throw the floater away to reveal a pure illustration or merge the floater with the drawing to retain some of the photographic quality.

Here is still another easy photo-manipulation technique that Painter will do. After opening the image you want to work on, choose the Water Brush in the Brushes palette and its Just Add Water variant. This tool will not brush on any color. Rather, it will only distort the existing pixels by blurring them as if they were dissolving. Be sure to begin with the Opacity in the Brush Controls palette set to around 30 percent or so. A setting of 100 percent completely blurs the image, like the Smudge tool does in Photoshop.

Left, a surface texture has been applied to the photo. Tools such as the Chalks and Pastels will respond to the texture by only putting paint on the tops of the ridges, allowing some of the photo to show through.

Below, the final image was brought back into Photoshop for a number of final adjustments.

The original image was scanned into Photoshop and given a basic clean-up.

The photo transformed by Painter's Water Brush.

This is the Brushes palette in its collapsed form. Even when collapsed there are seven pop-down menus, most of which each call up several more control dialog boxes. Painter offers absolute control over virtually everything.

TECHNICAL AND BUSINESS INFORMATION

FINDIT

Most file searching schemes are only able to locate items that are on some part of that active system. Wouldn't it be nice to have the search engine find a file whether it's on your computer or stored on a disk someplace? How about if I told you that there is such a utility and it's free? Well, if you bought a Zip or Jazz drive but never bothered to look at or even install the software that came with it, then you already have it.

The utility is called Findit. It catalogs every disk and CD when it is removed from the computer. It also catalogs every internal and external hard drive when it is shut down. Since the bigger internal drives can take some time cataloging and since you already have search engines for them, you may want to instruct Findit's prefs to catalog only the removable disks. To find a file, simply open the utility, plug in a few key words, and hit search. Findit will tell you which disk the file is on. All the files and folders on the named disk can be viewed.

PAINT ALCHEMY

Paint Alchemy, by MetaCreations, is a plug-in program that does a really wonderful thing. Although it can be a little slow at times, the results can be worth the wait. At the heart of the program is a series of PICT file brushes. These brushes apply a texture to the image based on their shape. The quality of the texture is also controlled by five control palettes: Brush, Color, Size, Angle, and Transparency. Each of these palettes is bristling with sliders and pop-up menus, which gives you an almost dizzying amount of control. Add to that the fact that you can easily make your own brushes by making new PICT file shapes in Photoshop. The variations are limitless. The two files of the bottles on the next page show a before and after.

Paint Alchemy comes with dozens of pre-set combinations. When you hit upon a combination of settings that you like, it can be saved and named for future use. A preview window allows you to try many combinations of settings quickly before hitting the Apply button.

If you save and name many custom filters, you might consider backing up the entire plug-in, complete with prefs. If you suffered a crash, you could reload the saved program with all the custom settings and brushes intact. This little bit of wisdom applies to any program whose custom settings would be difficult or time-consuming to replace.

Findit, by Iomega, is a practical little utility.

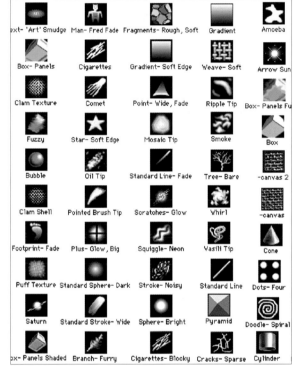

Paint Alchemy applies its magic through brushes like these. Since they are only PICT files, making your own is easy.

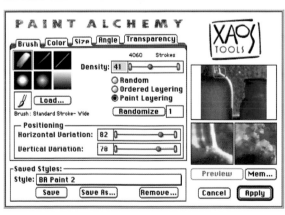

Each of Paint Alchemy's five windows is bristling with controls. If you come up with a combination of settings you like even a little, save them and name the settings. It will be added to the library of presets.

The original scan.

The possibilities are literally endless. Some combinations of settings really distort the image quite heavily while others, like this one, are more subtle.

FOTOQUOTE

This program, fotoQuote from Cradoc Corporation, has nothing at all to do with editing images. If you need a price for an image, however, this little program can be really helpful. The program was designed to be a stock photo pricing guide, but I find it very useful for pricing assigned work

as well. The prices the program gives you are actually ranges. For example, it will tell you that a specific usage will generally fetch between $1200 and $1800 with an average of $1500. There are also several quantifiers such as "Computer Enhanced" or "Aerial," which, when checked, usually mean to adjust the price upward.

Let's say clients call and ask you to do an image for an ad. The image will be of their product, orbiting around the earth. You're thinking, "Okay, a shoot, a few scans, a stock shot or a stock CD, some computer time—it should cost about $X." Then the clients inform you that the image will also appear on a small poster with a print run of five thousand, an invitation to a corporate event, a trade show booth, and five other things. No problem. Plug all the information for each use into fotoQuote, total the numbers, and there's your starting point. I say starting point because fotoQuote never pegs you to a hard and fast number. Rather, it will give you a low, high, and average price for the criteria you provide.

One of fotoQuote's nicest features for newcomers to the photography business is its coach-

fotoQuote v2.0

Advertising – National Magazine $ $2,155

Click on the camera for more information about this category.

Size	Rights Granted	Press Run
1/4 Page	One-Time Non-Exclusive	Under 250k
1/2 Page		250k – 500k
3/4 Page	RIGHTS : ONE TIME NON-EXCLUSIVE in one version only.	500k - 1 Million
Full Page		1 – 3 Million
Double Page		3 – 5 Million
Inside Cover		5 – 10 Million
Back Cover	Value Added Factors (Selected)...	10 – 20 Million
Gatefold		Over 20 Million

Coach Tips	
Usage Tips	This usage for Advertising – National Magazine will probably be priced between $1,616 and $3,232. The average price is $2,155.
Steps – Outline	
Partial Covers & Ads	Hold on to your seat and buckle up. You probably won't get many opportunities to negotiate this type of usage, and you want to get it right the first time. Chances are you'll be negotiating with the best, so do your homework thoroughly.
Multiple Insertions	
Documentation	
Improvising Prices	
Steps to a Sale	

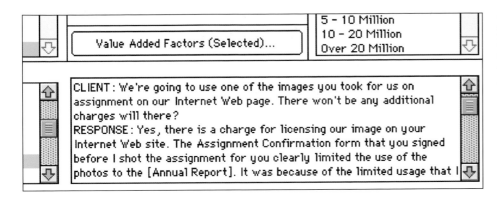

FotoQuoto even gives
you phone scripts to
help guide you through
conversations with
"budget-minded"
clients.

ing section. It will tell you how to place your price within the range of prices, why the price is as high or as low as it is, and other pertinent information. There is even a section called "Phone Scripts" where a conversation between a determined, penny-pinching client and a photographer with all the right answers is simulated. This section will help veterans as well if they find themselves bidding on a project that is outside their area of expertise.

NORTON UTILITIES

The smart ones buy Norton Utilities right away. I, of course, didn't get Norton until my first computer's hard drive was a fragmented mess. The Speed Disk portion of the program fixed me right up by optimizing the drive.

When you first begin saving files to your computer, the hard drive looks like the illustration at center right. After months of adding and deleting files, it may get to looking like the illustration below it. If your hard drive is fragmented and mostly full, saving a new large file might require that your computer break it up and store the pieces all over the place. This makes opening and closing the file slower. What Speed Disk does is to rewrite all the files back into one contiguous block and erase the free space.

I have heard some people advocating the frequent use of Speed Disk to keep all drives "defragged." My own experience is that overuse of Speed Disk occasionally results in small kinks and flaws in files. The most obvious is a bar of bright color, several pixels wide, that runs all the way across an image. The few times this happened to me I was able to fix the image with the Rubber Stamp tool, but it was unnerving to say the least. Everything in moderation.

Norton does a lot more than just optimize hard drives. In fact, the best known part of the program

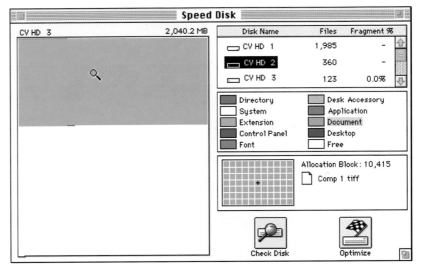

A newly optimized drive sports one contiguous block of data and another block of free space.

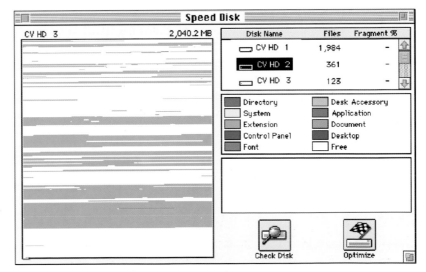

This is a graphic representation of a drive that has had many files written, thrown away, written again, and so on. This fragmented condition slows things down.

Norton's Disk Doctor swarms all over your drive looking for problems. When one is found, a course of action is recommended. Usually this is fixing the problem. A complete report can be viewed, saved, or printed.

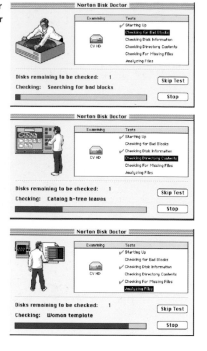

may be Disk Doctor. If you are having difficulties with your computer, Disk Doctor is a good place to start. It will run a series of diagnostics and if it comes across a problem, it will describe it and ask you if you want to fix it. If for some reason the problem can't be fixed, it will tell you. When the entire process is complete, Disk Doctor provides you with a detailed report of what was found and fixed.

Have you ever thrown a file away and then wanted it back? Of course, the file isn't really gone. The directory has just been changed indicating to your computer that the space once occupied by the file is now available again. If nothing has been written over your file, the UnErase feature of Norton will almost always be able to retrieve it. I'm always surprised to see all the other junk that Norton finds still lurking in my drive when I use this utility.

QUICKEYS

If you hate going up to the menu bar and love keyboard shortcuts, then do I have a program for you. QuicKeys is just what the doctor ordered, but a lot less expensive than his or her bills. Granted, the Actions palette in Photoshop does allow you to generate your own key-driven shortcuts for many tasks, but not all. And it only allows you to use the F keys. After you've spent those, then what do you do?

QuicKeys picks up where Photoshop's Actions palette leaves off. Key combinations or single keys, other than the F keys, can be used. As in the Actions palette, single tasks or whole sequences can be recorded. In addition to key commands though, QuicKeys will let you create buttons to activate your commands or even rows of buttons called Tool Bars. Voice-activated commands are even possible, provided you have voice-recognition software and hardware already installed.

The real beauty is that all of these features can be made to work for your other programs as well, not just Photoshop. QuicKeys will let you make application-specific shortcuts or universal shortcuts that will work in just about any program. It will let you double up on application-specific key commands. Option-T could be one thing in Photoshop, another in Live Picture, and still another in Bryce.

One small thing to watch for is making universal shortcuts that are activated by typing a single letter. I wanted to make a shortcut with the letter M key. When it was hit, my Monitors control panel would pop up, the number of colors switched from wherever they were to millions, and then the panel would close again. "Wow. 'M' for millions. This is great." I thought. A few days later I tried to change the name of a file. You can guess what happened when I needed to type the letter M into the new file name.

Again, the above selection of programs is, of course, only a tiny fraction of what is out there. I got a little program-happy for a while and dabbled with other monster titles such as Director, Premier, and Infini-D, great programs all. In the end, it seemed as though I was spreading myself too thin. I decided to focus and stick with what is important to me.

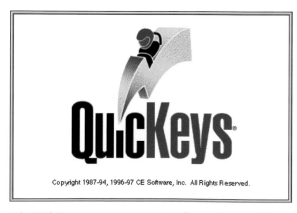

Using QuicKeys to create macros can really speed up repetitive tasks.

BOY WITH BELL
WORKING WITH PAINTER

THIS IMAGE was done primarily in Painter 5.0. The look, although rich and painterly, was very easy to achieve. Full knowledge of this program is not a must. Even if you have only played with Painter once or twice, it will take you only seconds to set up the program to do this technique. What basically happens is that a source image is cloned and brushed on top of another. A crude version of this technique could be done within Photoshop by taking a Snapshot of one image and, with the Rubber Stamp set to the "From Snapshot mode," brushing it onto another image. The only thing missing from this method is the degree of control over the texture and the quality of the brush itself. Painter does this very well.

In addition to Painter, I used two photographs, a drawing tablet, and a bit of Photoshop. The shot of the boy was from my files. The photo was taken on Monhegan Island, Maine. The reddish texture onto which he was "painted" is a photograph of a sheet of textured wallpaper that was backlit. Both images were scanned into Photoshop and then cleaned up.

The colors in the parchment image were pushed quite heavily from the original pale beige toward a deep, leathery red. The colors in the shot of the boy were also pushed, especially the blues and greens in the bell. I knew that the reds of the parchment would be breaking through and that the blues and greens had to be strong enough to hold up. The sky was made to look much more blue than the original.

Since the bell image needed to fit onto the parchment with some room to spare, they were sized accordingly. The parchment was 4 x 5 inches at 600 dpi and the bell was 3½ x 4½ inches at 600 dpi. They were both saved as Photoshop files, which Painter can open. I worked at that resolution because I wanted to have a 4 x 5-inch chrome made from the file.

With the images ready, Photoshop was closed and Painter was launched. An army of palettes

greets you when you open Painter, but only a few are needed for this technique. The Advanced Controls, Art Materials, and Color Set palettes can be closed immediately. Once the Brush tool is chosen from the Tools palette, that one can be closed as well. The Brushes palette is where you decide what style the brush will imitate—oil brush, pencil, chalk, pen and ink, and so on. Among these choices is one called Cloners. The

The original photo was cleaned up in Photoshop prior to its being opened in Painter.

Photographers are always on the lookout for new textures with which to work. This photo is of a piece of wallpaper. The reds were strengthened to complement the blues and greens of the bell.

Painter's icon representing the Cloner tool.

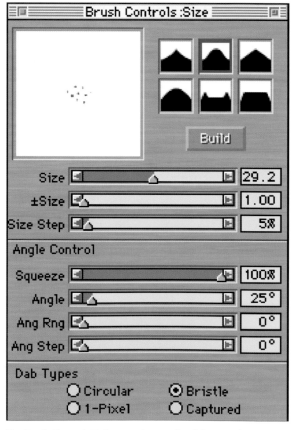

The Brush Size palette is a good example of the complete control one has over every aspect of working in Painter. The Bristle radio button is checked in the Dab Type section at the bottom for this image.

The Brushes palette is a busy place.

The parchment file is made the active image and set to Screen mode. This is the same as Full-screen mode in Photoshop where scroll bars and other files are hidden.

In the Brush Controls palette, the brush size and Dab Type are set. With the Circular Brush button checked, the resulting stroke looks the same as the Photoshop brushes. I checked the Bristle button and left it there for the entire cloning process. The bristle brush makes a stippled, streaky brush stroke.

You may be sick of hearing about brushes by now but with Painter, it is all in the brushes and there is one more palette for adjusting the quality of the brush strokes. This is the Controls palette and it sets the opacity of the stroke. I like to set the opacity around 60 percent for this technique and let the layers build up. If the same area is gone over enough times, full opacity is reached and the image onto which you are painting is completely covered. You may find that certain critical parts of an image such as eyes need this kind of opacity.

sole purpose of this tool is to allow you to paint the contents of one file onto another. It is chosen by clicking the Cloners icon or by choosing it from the first pop-down menu.

The second pop-down menu contains choices that further describe the characteristics of the chosen brush. For my image, I started with Chalk Cloner, brought out the details with the Soft Cloner, and used the Straight Cloner sparingly. Most of the other choices distort too heavily for my taste. The name Soft Cloner initially led me to think that the cloned image would never be as sharp as the original. I was afraid it would have some distortion. In fact, it only means that the brush has a soft edge. The Brushes palette can be closed for a while.

The next step is to use the Clone from Source command found under File in the main menu. All open files are shown here and once the source image is chosen, the cloning can begin. The image of the boy was painted onto the parchment file, so this is the one that was chosen as the source image. It must remain open during the cloning process.

You could try this type of image with a mouse instead of a drawing tablet. The brush strokes would not fade in and out as with a pressure-sensitive stylus, but with a deft, artistic touch you could get something pleasing. The tablet and stylus do bring it to the next level, though, and give things a finer, more polished look. It's also more intuitive and just plain fun.

Let the cloning begin. I usually make a few big practice strokes to see where things are in relation to the "canvas" image. If you want the brush strokes to follow the contours of the cloned image, you need to do this to get your bearings. Since Painter lets you adjust the preferences to have up to thirty-two consecutive undos, you can do a lot of "seeing where things are" and still be able to start over easily. Clicking back and forth between images is also helpful.

The image of the boy was lightly scratched in overall with a larger brush. The Cloner style was Chalk Cloner with a Bristle brush. The Chalk Cloner sprays down color from the source image but distorts it as it does so. The idea for this first layer of paint is to rough in the major elements and blocks of color while still leaving plenty of parchment showing through.

The image was gone over several more times and areas of importance were stroked with progressively smaller brushes. If you don't change the brush size at all, the image will end up looking flat and will seem like something is missing. When enough color had been blocked in, I switched to the Soft Cloner.

This tool will begin to bring out the photographic likeness of the source image. Again, the brushes arc worked large to small. Important areas, such as the boy's hand and edges of the bell, were emphasized.

When the cloning is complete, don't just hit Save. Use the Save As command to make a new file. Just hitting Save writes over the "canvas" file, in this case the Parchment file, which should be preserved for another "painting." After saving, bring the image back into Photoshop.

For the soft edges, I took the Square Marquee, selected all but the last quarter inch around the perimeter of the image, and feathered this selection to 35 pixels. After using the Select Inverse command, the background was set to white and the selection was deleted. I liked the fade to white but wanted more of it so the Canvas Size palette was opened and a half inch more white was added all around.

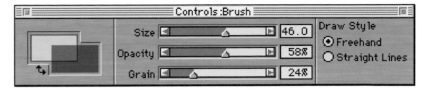

Because so much red and orange is showing through the blues and greens of the photo, the result looks muddy. Using Selective Color, I pulled quite a bit of cyan out of the reds and yellows. The whites, blues, and greens were also cleaned up by pulling some of their respective color opposites out. More black was added to the blacks. After the Selective Color adjustment, a little contrast was applied with Curves.

Art and commercial photography have moved closer together than ever before. The style of this image is quite different from many of my others. While I feel fortunate to be in this business at a time when art buyers will accept a wider variety of styles, I don't try to mix styles in a single portfolio. The collage, illustrations, and altered-reality images are shown and promoted separately.

Setting the Opacity to 50 percent or so is a good place to begin with this style of image.

The first few strokes with the Chalk Cloner are being put down here. Go slowly. It's a fun process. Why rush?

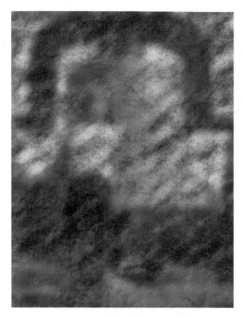

Here the Chalk Cloner has put down enough paint. Switching now to the Soft Cloner will begin to bring out the finer detail.

The Soft Cloner reproduces the finer details of the source image. Hit the areas of most important detail first, leaving plenty of swaths of rougher brushwork in between for a painterly look.

The cloning is finished and the image is now back in Photoshop here. Extra canvas area has been added prior to softening the edges of the image.

The final image has had both color and total adjustments made to overcome the muted qualities the cloning process imparts.

CHAPTER EIGHT

PROFESSIONAL CONSIDERATIONS
RUNNING A SUCCESSFUL BUSINESS

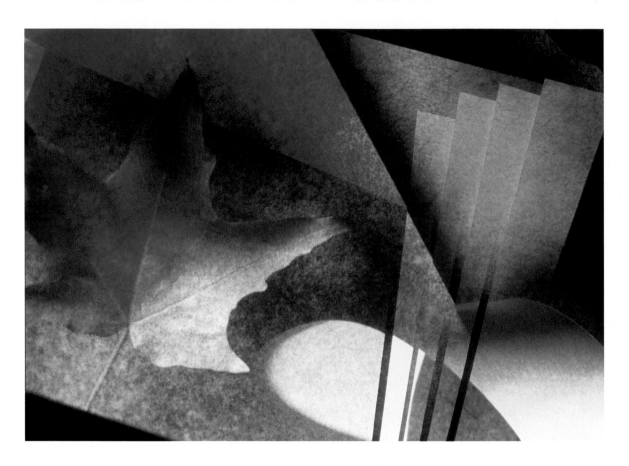

"Nothing in the world can take the place of persistence. Talent will not: Nothing is more common than unsuccessful men with talent. Genius will not: Unrewarded genius is almost a proverb. Education will not: The world is full of educated derelicts. Persistence and determination alone are omnipotent."

ANONYMOUS

I REMEMBER the first time I assisted another photographer. At the end of the first day, he said, "Are you really sure you want to do this? It's a difficult way to make a living."

"Was I that bad?"

"You were fine. I just want to make sure you know what you're getting into."

I forged ahead in ignorant bliss, unencumbered by any knowledge of the realities of the business of photography. How could I know? In fact, it was probably better that I didn't.

If you've already got a thriving business going, incorporating the business aspects of electronic photography will be a natural progression. It's only the learning curve of image manipulation that will slow you down. You'll have plenty of new decisions to make, such as placing your images with stock photo agencies, showing your work digitally, such as on a CD or even a Web site, pricing, reps, insurance, and more. Those last few are not considerations that are exclusive to the digital arena, but are important topics none the less.

STOCK PHOTOGRAPHY AND DIGITAL IMAGING

Having digital capability is a great asset to many photographers, including those who are interested in selling their images as stock photography. Images already in your files that might not sell in their original state can be modified or added to other shots and made into winners. Putting a perfect moonrise over an otherwise average cityscape can now be done easily. Making a series of collages of financial elements, such as coins and monetary symbols, could keep you busy for quite a while.

The only real limiting factor is that the image you come up with should justify the cost of outputting a good chrome such as an LVT (Live Valve Technologies) of Fire 1000. At the time of this writing, the cost of having a 4 x 5 chrome made ranges between $125 and $200, while an 8 x 10 Fire 1000 runs between $150 and $300. With a little extra work, four 4 x 5s can be gotten from one 8 x 10, bringing the cost to around $50 per 4 x 5. I have heard from a few photographers who have been able to get their stock agency to accept digital files, passing on the burden and expense of making the chromes to them. I hope this catches on.

If you don't have and/or can't shoot a spectacular element needed for an assignment, you may use somebody else's. Stock photography is a natural choice in this circumstance. The quality and diversity of what's available is better than it has ever been. If you need brilliant shots of Stonehenge by tomorrow, it may be the only choice.

The downside to using stock comes up when your image gets reused or sold. If there is a stock photo embedded somewhere in the shot, things get complicated. For their one element, the stock houses will ask for a fee equal to or greater than the total the client is willing to pay for the entire image. That doesn't leave much for you.

My images are placed with The Stock Market and I have been very happy with the arrangement. Shots that use other people's stock elements within them, however, can't be placed

You could buy a royalty-free stock CD and get a collection of sunsets but why not shoot your own? It's good, clean, tax-deductible fun and your images are probably better anyway.

Consistency in advertising is more important than fretting over which book is the right one or whether direct mail is better than the books. Choose a medium and stick to it. I have been inconsistent in the past and have learned my lesson.

there. Happily, these images are often so specific that it's not an issue. They could never sell as stock images.

If an image looks as though it is going to have potential sales beyond the original use, I find it best to put in whatever effort is necessary to keep the image "clean." This usually means shooting all the elements myself, even if I have to do a bit more work than the original fee might justify.

When you don't want to do that extra work and you also don't want to go through a stock house, royalty-free stock may be your last option. The key word is "may." There is still a lot of mediocrity to be found. The available choices in any one category are much more limited than what the stock houses can offer. Still, if they happen to have the element you need, and you can enhance the element to match the quality of what you are working on, then perhaps it's a workable solution for you. The few times I've pulled an element from one of these disks it's left a bad taste in my mouth.

I am against selling or leasing images to companies that produce royalty-free stock disks. I think that photographers who do this are mortgaging their future for the present. They are shooting their own industry in the foot. I know the popularity of royalty-free stock disks was inevitable and will continue to grow, but don't look for any of my images on a royalty-free CD. I won't do it.

SELLING YOURSELF

As Will Rogers said, "Even if you are on the right track, you'll get run over if you just sit there."

Advertising pays. Actually, first you pay, *then* it pays. It takes time. Don't buy a page in a source book, such as *The Black Book* or *New York Gold,* and expect things to take off immediately. The more people see your name around,

the more prospective clients will accept you as legitimate. Just when you feel that money spent on advertising is the equivalent of digging a big hole and throwing your money into it, the calls may really start to come in.

If you are able to get a designer to help you with the look of your pages, do so. You will not regret it. Most photographers seem to use the "more and bigger is better" style of page design. "Dead space? Who needs it?" we say. Thumb quickly through a few source books and see where you pause most frequently. I find it's not generally the pages that are totally covered in ink.

An alternative to the source books is placing an ad in one or more of the trade magazines that go out to ad agencies and design firms. These include magazines like *Graphis, How,* and *Communication Arts.* The advantage is that you will likely be one of only a few photographers with an ad. If the image is strong, you *will* be noticed. Try to get placement near the front of the magazine.

Direct mail is another powerful advertising tool. In fact, if you forced me to use only one method of advertising, this would be it, despite the time-consuming nature of it. A strong mailer, sent to area agencies and designers, and followed up with a phone call, yields results. The mailer can be reprints of a source book page, a piece printed just for the mailing, or one of the digital options below. When sending to new local names, try mailing a small batch at a time. That way you can really focus on the follow-up calls and time them for just a day or two after the piece has been received.

The bottom line is that advertising works. The most successful self-promoters don't really ever stop. They continue pushing even when they are busy.

PRESENTING YOUR PORTFOLIO DIGITALLY

Traditional photographers have several options when it comes to putting together a portfolio. We as digital photographers can utilize all of these and a few more. Here are some electronic options.

Floppy Disk

Instead of, or in addition to, sending a printed card through the mail, send a small cross section of your work on a floppy disk. There are several simple presentation programs, such as Proview, made for the task. With more complex programs, such as Director, it is possible to fit a half dozen images, fades, and transitions, and even a bit of looped sound on a single floppy.

As a finishing touch, give your disk a custom icon. Here's how. Create the icon in Photoshop and save it. Open the folder where the saved file is. Under View in the regular desktop menu bar, select By Icon. Click on the file once to select it. Hit Command-I. At the top of the Information window you will see the icon again. Click on it and a black outline will appear around it. Hit Command-C for Copy. Now insert the disk that will get the new icon. Click on it once and hit Command-I again. Click on the icon of the disk to put the black outline around it. Hit Command-V for Paste. The new icon is pasted over the old one.

CD-ROM

If prospective clients are interested in your abbreviated portfolio on disk, they can be sent the standard portfolio or the full portfolio on CD. It sure is easier to drop one of these into a FedEx envelope than to send the full-sized book. At 640 megs, a CD has enough space to contain even the most complex presentations. Video, elaborate sound, and "about the artist" sections will all fit easily.

There are two routes to take once your presentation is built. You can either make the CDs as you need them on your desktop CDR machine or have quantity runs done professionally. I would recommend this second route for any sizable mailing. The cost per unit will be lower, the

Lightning Catchers   Info

Lightning Catchers

Kind: Photoshop® JPEG file
Size: 236K on disk (241,139 bytes used)

Where: CV HD: Portfolio:

Created: Tue, Jul 29, 1997, 10:57 AM
Modified: Tue, Jul 29, 1997, 10:57 AM
Version: n/a

Comments:

☐ **Locked**   ☐ **Stationery pad**

Click once on a file or folder to select it. After hitting Command-I to get the Info window open, click once on the icon in the window. A black bar apperars around the icon. Hit Command-C to copy it to the clipboard. In the target file or folder's Info window, select the Icon again and Paste (Command-V).

The ability to write your own CDs is well worth the price of the drive. Archiving images, sending out portfolios on disk, and moving large files are a few of the uses.

disks will look much better, and, perhaps most importantly, your time can be spent on other tasks.

Putting together a CD is not cheap—even if you produce it yourself with a program like Director. I had one produced for $3500, which is relatively cheap (a friend did the Director work). The price included the Director work, a run of 500 silk-screened CDs, and jewel boxes.

Web Site

You don't have to be a digital artist to have a Web site, of course. You don't even have to have a Web site. Space on someone else's can be rented inexpensively. There are several sites that charge a small fee to artists wanting to post some of their work. Having your own site does have its advantages—prestige, control over how much work is shown, additional pages about you, or prints you may have for sale. You can also upload images to the server and have someone else such as a client download them. They just need to get the access codes from you. This is called File Transfer Protocol, or FTP. Files that are a bit too large to e-mail can be sent this way.

A photographer I know has done a few jobs where the client needed images taken and then uploaded to his Web site the same afternoon. He rented a 35mm digital camera, set up his computer at the location, and posted the images right from the location. If you find yourself in this situation, charge for the extra footwork.

Directing people to your Web site certainly helps confirm your status as a digital expert. A less obvious advantage to having a site is the ability to transfer files through the server that supports it.

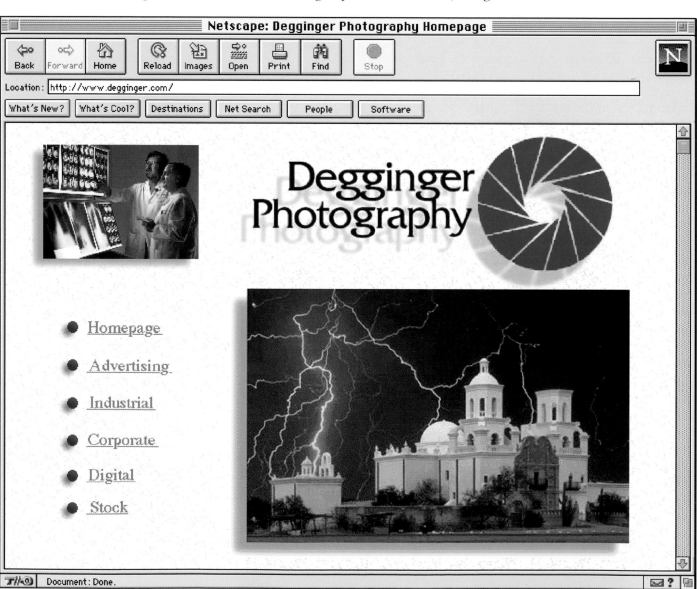

E-mail capability is rapidly becoming more accepted and expected. Being able to send low-res comps and images for a fraction of overnight delivery charges is a real plus.

E-mail

How about creating a promotional piece and then, instead of having it printed and mailed at great expense, e-mailing it to prospective clients? Make it once and send it over and over. This becomes increasingly feasible as more and more people include an e-mail address on their business cards and stationery.

Sending low-res comps by way of e-mail to a client a few time zones away is fast and inexpensive. The money you would save by avoiding one or two FedEx deliveries a month would more than pay for being online. It has also become de rigueur for digitally literate photographers to have Internet access. The limitation is that sending files much larger than a few megs is ponderous. Sending an image of any size to an AOL (America Online) address is also problematic.

I currently have two clients that e-mail me, rather than call me, with their intentions of hiring me for a job. I see more and more e-mail usage as time goes by.

Digital Prints

Traditional C prints are expensive. First there is the interneg, and then the print itself. The cost of the interneg isn't an issue if many prints are made at one time. Digital prints can be made directly from a file. At half the cost, they're a bargain in small quantities. Dye-subs, Fujix, and Digital Cs are a few of the many print types. Most service bureaus make the first two. Contact Dugal in New York City for Digital Cs.

If you like to laminate your prints, you may want to avoid using Dye-subs, which can only be cold-laminated. This results in a lamination with a slightly raised area above the print (hot laminations are flat).

THE IMPORTANCE OF BEING DETAIL-ORIENTED

If you are the sort of person who is a bit casual about how you go about things (I was), working on the computer every day will cure you of this in a hurry. Following procedures and paying almost obsessive-compulsive attention to detail really are a must. I'm afraid you really do have to "sweat the small stuff."

Being orderly is really to save your own sanity. If files and disks are not kept in order, you will waste a lot of time searching for things that are "around here somewhere." Orderliness also means that you have a dedicated, inviolate partition for scratch disk space, that the desktop is rebuilt once a week (hold down the Command and Option keys on start-up), and that CMYKs are always saved separately from the image in layers. It means that Disk Doctor or the equivalent is run periodically, that major changes by the client are saved as sep files or layers (lest they change their mind), and that elements, layered images, CMYKs, and low-res images all get their own folders.

Procedures, the predetermined way that you approach each assignment, are for someone else—the fickle client. Here's an example. The client, let's call him Mr. Punkinhead, knows that you can make changes to the file at any time and will certainly ask you to do so many times. Mr. P. may even ask you to make changes that seem easy to him but cause you unreasonable amounts of work. If a price for the job has already been established, things could get ugly. What you need is a set of procedures that Mr. P. gets a copy of before any work begins. Establishing times for sign-offs and putting a price tag on certain changes will put a stop to the endless "adjust-

As the anonymous saying goes, "If you chase two rabbits, both will escape."

Creating images on the computer can be intoxicating. Once you've gotten a handle on Photoshop, Live Picture, and a few other staple programs, you may find yourself tempted to dabble in multimedia or video. It's fun to explore. You may even decide that one of these areas is more appealing to you than photography. If you try to make money doing them all you are sure to fail. Stay focused. Don't try to learn too many programs. You may find yourself becoming a slave to them.

ments." The sign-offs might work this way. All parties view and sign off on the final sketch of the image before any photography takes place. The photographed elements are looked at and everyone signs off. A low-res image is put together and approved before the high-res work begins, and so on. Generally, going backward costs, especially going backward from the high-res stage.

PROFESSIONAL REPRESENTATION

Should you have a rep or not have a rep? That is the question. A rep fields the phone calls, does most of the price negotiating, sends out and receives the portfolios, and handles the billing. That work represents (no pun intended) a lot of time. How much is that time worth to you? 25 percent of the fee? 30 percent? Some reps are nonexclusive and only take a piece of what they bring in. Some reps want 30 percent of everything they bring in and all of your house accounts as well. Now that's rich. These big guns rub elbows with the right people, though. Look through the books at the pages of the guys with the big-name reps and you will see some images made for some big-name accounts. That's the trade off and probably not a bad one at that.

INSURANCE

Sitting in front of a screen making images does not seem like the sort of occupation that would require a lot of insurance. But before you cancel your policies remember that models and clients

Archiving anything to magnetic media like Zip disks or SyQuest cartridges is risky. I have had more than one refuse to open because of a disk error with all the files lost. It's enough to make you run out and buy a CD read-write machine, which is exactly what I did. Finals, CMYKs, and important elements are now saved to a CD. If you don't want to spend the $400 to $1200 for the machine, service bureaus will make these CDs for you. It won't take but four or five CDs, though, before you surpass the cost of buying the machine itself. They earn their keep.

Trade shows are an entertaining way for you to keep up with what's out there technology-wise. Things are changing at a disturbing pace. Products on display at these shows are often prototypes of what is to come, not samples of what can be had today. The guys at the booths won't volunteer this too quickly. They'll have a whole rap all prepared for you. The trick is to have some tough questions ready for them. Often learning what a piece of gear or software *won't* do is as informative as learning what it does do. Make sure you ask when the item you are interested in will *really* ship.

will still come to your studio and you will still go on location.

These situations obviously call for insurance. The more subtle risks can be just as damaging. What if a package containing one-of-a-kind merchandise, a portfolio, or chromes from a stock house gets lost or destroyed, not by you, but by the delivery company. Are you covered? An uninsured FedEx package that gets lost might net you $100 if you are nice; $500 if you really kick and scream. Does your current policy cover the difference in a situation like this? Find out. While you're at it, be nice to your agent. Your agent may be able to advocate for you if the insurance company is on the fence about whether to pay up. If you do want to send and insure a single package with FedEx, be sure not to put it in a FedEx Letter or FedEx Pak. These two containers are only covered for a maximum of $500.

Reps send portfolios out all the time. They would go broke if they bought insurance from the overnight delivery companies every time they sent out a package. Being covered for loss on the general insurance policy is much cheaper. You won't send out nearly as many packages as a rep, but this idea will still save you money.

I have never had to buy job insurance, but I know people who have. This one-time insurance covers you in the event that a job that would be really expensive to redo has to get redone. For example, let's say you go on location with several top models. Between airfare, hotel, models, and film, you spend a lot of money. If the lab had a bad day and all your film is ruined, the client would not be pleased. The job insurance wouldn't compensate you for the lost time, but the expenses would be covered.

PRICING

I've got one last topic to cover and I'm afraid it's one that makes me rant and rave. The topic is pricing and how it relates to established photographers. When a potential client calls and asks you to bid on a large or high-profile job, for God's sake, keep your chin (and your prices) up. You have spent years learning to be a professional photographer or illustrator, you've invested in a lot of expensive equipment, you've learned another skill—digital imaging—and you've invested in some more pricey equipment. Don't give it away! The numbers some people offer up are unbelievable. I bid on a job recently. It was a double-page, full-bleed image to be printed in major magazines for the national launch of a new product. The image was to have a product shot, a landscape shot, and about 40 to 50 people, some models and the rest, extras. Bids were coming in as low as $3500. This was insanity.

In the good old days of straight photography, you took the picture, handed your client the film, and sent in the invoice. Now you may find yourself converting your files to CMYK, meeting with printers, and adjusting the files if the match prints don't look right. This extra work requires your expertise and shouldn't come free.

Another thing that some photographers seem all too ready to do is to give away the copyright. They shoot the job and just hand the film to the clients, allowing them to reuse the imagery whenever and wherever they please with no additional fee. Some clients expect this and, additionally, expect that you will never use the images anywher else as well. This is called "work for hire" and you should try to avoid it like the plague unless you are being paid accordingly. I know this is easier said than done. In many areas, such as in small business-to-business advertising or when working for companies directly, it is very hard to avoid this topic. If you need help in setting up pricing, there are several sources:

FotoQuote

Get yourself a copy of the software program called fotoQuote. As described on page 130, this program is a terrific guide with lots of coaching, phone scripts, and the like.

Printed Guides

The American Society of Media Photographers (ASMP) and similar groups have printed guides on pricing standards that they will send. You may not always agree with their numbers, but at least it's a starting point.

Advice from Peers

Call your peers and ask them. You probably have at least one friend in your field who has more experience than you do. Peers will certainly have some good advice to share.

THE LAST WORD

It's anyone's guess as to where digital photography will take us in the years ahead. At less than twenty years old, it is an industry still in its infancy. Clearly, it will continue to rapidly gain both in acceptance and in the numbers of practitioners. I don't think, though, that it will steamroll over film-based photography any time soon. A peaceful coexistence seems the most likely scenario for some years. A major breakthrough in the quality and cost of the CCD chips that comprise the heart of most scanners and digital cameras might hasten the "conversion." Personally, I hope film is always around and a "conversion" never fully takes place. For many situations, film is still the best, safest, and cheapest way to store an image.

I would like to tell you that being a professional photographer in the digital age is better and easier than ever. Unfortunately, that doesn't seem to be the case. The truth is that it is more difficult now than ever. The increasing availability of stock photography and images on CD have impacted the volume of assignment work. All the more reason to push your efforts in the direction of stock. Some work has been pulled in-house by agencies with digital departments. Mediocrity seems to be accepted much too frequently these days in the name of saving a buck. Chopping budgets is almost fashionable to some people. Innovative, dedicated, and persistent photographers will survive and thrive, though. Those qualities always stand out.

The rules of engagement may be changing, but so too are the tools. Never before have photographers had so many possible styles and mediums to choose from in expressing their artistic vision.

SELECTED BIBLIOGRAPHY

Fraser, Bruce, and David Blanter. *Real World Photoshop 4: Industrial Strength Production Techniques.* Berkeley: Peachppit Press, 1997.

Gerber, Michael E. *The E-Myth Revisited: Why Most Small Businesses Don't Work and What to Do About It.* New York: Harper Business, 1995.

Karson, Josh. *Live Picture Revealed.* Indianapolis: Hayden Books, 1996.

Kasai, Akira, and Russell Sparkman. *The Essentials of Digital Photography.* Indianapolis: New Riders, 1997.

McClelland, Deke, and Ted Padova. *Macworld Photoshop 4 Bible.* Foster City, CA: IDG Books, 1997.

Threinen-Pendarvis, Cher. *The Painter 5 Wow! Book.* Berkeley: Peachpit Press, 1998.

INDEX